# The Marine Life of Ningaloo Marine Park & Coral Bay

By Ann Storrie & Sue Morrison

Contributor Bill Brogan

GOVERNMENT OF WESTERN AUSTRALIA

DEPARTMENT OF
Conservation
AND LAND MANAGEMENT
Conserving the nature of WA

# Contents

# Introduction

The Ningaloo Marine Park protects one of Australia's most important tracts of reef. It is unique because of its proximity and accessibility to the coast, and for its prolific marine life. It is the only place in the world where our largest fish, the whale shark, can be predictably found and studied. It supports more than 500 species of fish, 250 known species of corals and about 600 species of molluscs. Green turtles have extensive rookeries inside the reef, dugong feed on seagrasses within the lagoons and humpback whales migrate close to the coast. It is an area where tropical and temperate waters mix and the rugged, arid beauty of the Cape Range National Park provides a stark background to this profusion of life under the waves.

The word Ningaloo is an Aboriginal word meaning a promontory. The Cape Range Peninsula is the promontory and the Ningaloo Reef runs parallel to its western coast. The reef extends for approximately 260 kilometres from North West Cape in the north (21° 47' S) to south of Amherst Point, south of Coral Bay (32° 34' S). It is a part barrier, part fringing reef system with reefs ranging from seven kilometres to less than 200 metres offshore (a barrier reef is separated from the coast by a wide expanse of water, whereas a fringing reef is separated from the coast only by a shallow lagoon). Several different ecosystems within these boundaries support a huge variety of marine life.

Lagoons between the shore and the reef are protected from strong oceanic swells. Here, sandy bottoms are interspersed with seagrass meadows and hard corals such as staghorn corals (*Acropora* species), which dominate the shallows of Coral Bay. In some areas a very shallow reef, known as a 'beach platform', lies right on the shore. It is often old, cemented coral that formed when the sea level was higher.

Beyond the lagoon is a reef flat, or 'back reef', a zone that often stretches for several hundred metres out to sea. It is usually shallow, and is washed by a strong surge of water flowing from the surf that breaks on its outer edge. This water brings essential nutrients and oxygen to corals that make use of the abundant sunlight on the reef flat and within the lagoons.

Left: *A variety of hard corals.*
*Photo - Sue Morrison*
Right: *Black-saddled toby (*Canthigaster valentini*).*
*Photo - Ann Storrie*

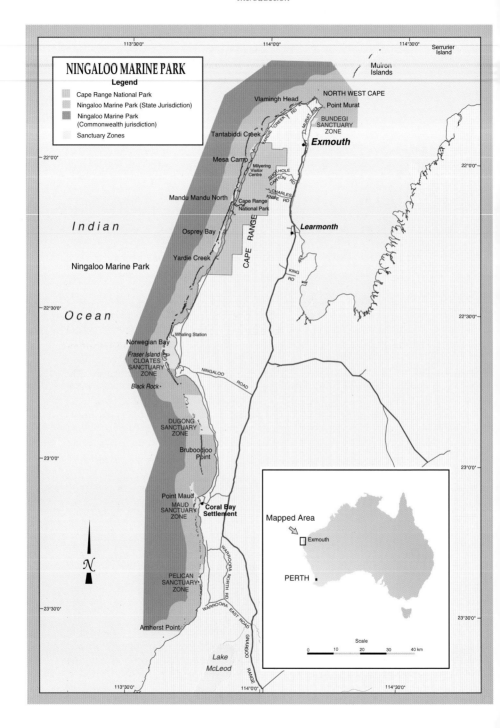

## NINGALOO MARINE PARK

**Legend**

- Cape Range National Park
- Ningaloo Marine Park (State Jurisdiction)
- Ningaloo Marine Park (Commonwealth jurisdiction)
- Sanctuary Zones

Passages, or breaks, in the reef flat occur every few kilometres. These are similar to creeks flowing through Cape Range on the land. Water flows through the channels with the changes in tide and the swells, and allows these areas to support an enormous array of marine life.

The outer edge of the reef flat drops off to a rocky bottom, 10 to 25 metres deep. This 'drop off' is often steep and has been weathered by constant swells that have formed caves, ledges and gullies along its length. Marine life is extremely diverse and prolific in this region, and includes many pelagic fish (those that spend most of their lives swimming in the open ocean) and turtles. From the drop-off, the bottom slopes gently for up to 40 kilometres offshore, where it is between 100 and 200 metres deep.

# Formation of Ningaloo Reef

Coral reefs have flourished in the Ningaloo region for thousands of years. Fossils found in the rock formations of Cape Range National Park are very similar to the present marine life of the Ningaloo Reef. Cape Range probably started forming about 15 million years ago, when sediments that had slowly been accumulating on the seabed, and cementing into rock, began to buckle upwards. This folding is a gradual process, with only a couple of millimetres of movement every 100 years.

The actual formation of the coral reef is quite a complex process. Though the primary building blocks of the reef are the coral animals, they depend on microscopic cellular plants called zooxanthellae for their energy and fast growth. Zooxanthellae live within the coral animal and enable the coral to grow and secrete calcium carbonate at a rate faster than it is destroyed by physical, chemical and biological processes. The living coral that is seen on the top of the reef is often only a few centimetres thick. Underneath is layer upon layer of solid limestone, or the calcium carbonate foundation. Other animals also contribute to the formation of the reef. Many types of algae secrete calcium carbonate, and the skeletal remains of other reef-dwelling animals contribute to the foundation.

An interesting aspect of Ningaloo Reef is that it occurs further south than would normally be expected for a tropical reef environment. The fact that its corals have grown and flourished in this latitude is due to a southward-flowing stream of tropical water that occurs off the Western Australian coast. This tropical stream was named the Leeuwin Current, after a Dutch vessel which explored the south-western coast of Australia in 1622. The current is a band of warm, low salinity water about 50 kilometres wide and up to 200 metres deep. It originates in the tropics and carries a variety of tropical marine species with it as it travels down the Western Australian coast.

The Leeuwin Current also brings many nutrients down from large mangrove systems further north. This, coupled with the arid conditions of the Cape Range, which produce little terrestrial run-off of water, may have contributed to the spectacular reef development.

The Ningaloo Reef is often compared with the Great Barrier Reef, but they are in fact totally different systems. The Great Barrier Reef extends from between 35 and 100 nautical miles out to sea. The Ningaloo Reef is located very close to shore, ranging from a few hundred metres to about seven to eight kilometres offshore. It is found further south, at the equivalent of the southernmost end of the Great Barrier Reef, and is a much smaller system. Nevertheless, the diversity of its corals and fish life match those of the Great Barrier Reef, largely because it is a meeting place of temperate and tropical waters and because of the influence of the Leeuwin Current. Another influential factor is that the continental shelf is relatively close to the coast at Ningaloo, ranging from about two nautical miles out to sea near the tip of North West Cape to about 20 nautical miles out to sea off Point Maud.

## Marine park status

The Ningaloo Reef has, for many years, been recognised as an important resource for tourism, fisheries and research for Western Australia. In 1987, the Ningaloo Marine Park was proclaimed by both the State and Commonwealth Governments, and it is managed by the Western Australian Department of Conservation and Land Management (CALM). The marine park includes nearly all of the reef system and encompasses more than 5000 square kilometres of ocean.

To cater for conservation and recreation within the Ningaloo Marine Park, CALM has separated the area into three management zones. These reflect the distribution of natural resources and separate potentially conflicting activities. Sanctuary zones are 'no take' areas where plants and animals must not be disturbed. They provide scientific benchmark areas with which to compare nearby exploited areas, and replenishment zones to restock these exploited areas. There are eight sanctuary zones, which make up 18 per cent of the park. Recreation zones are areas where recreational fishing is allowed, though commercial fishing is not permitted. They form 22 per cent of the park. The general use zone makes up the other 60 per cent of the area and provides for commercial and recreational uses consistent with conservation of natural resources.

*Ningaloo looking south. Photo - Garin Taylor*

*A soft coral (Carijoa multiflora) showing eight tentacles on each polyp, a characteristic of all soft corals. A thin layer of orange sponge grows over the main stem of the colony. Photo - Sue Morrison*

## Marine conservation in Western Australia

Ningaloo is part of a much larger marine park system in Western Australia. At present there are seven marine parks (the other five are at Marmion, Shoalwater Islands, Rowley Shoals, Swan Estuary, Shark Bay and Jurien Bay) and one marine nature reserve (at Hamelin Pool in Shark Bay). A specialist Marine Conservation Branch has been established within CALM to drive the establishment of a comprehensive marine reserve system and to provide policy, planning and scientific advice to help marine park managers carry out their work. In future, there are likely to be more new marine reserves declared than terrestrial reserves. In 1994, the Wilson Report, a pioneering report on marine conservation for Western Australia, recommended that about 70 marine regions around the State's coastline be considered for classification as marine reserves so that their conservation values can be safeguarded forever. One of the areas under consideration is a southern extension of the Ningaloo Marine Park.

# History

## Aboriginal history

Aboriginal people inhabited the Cape Range Peninsula for at least 30,000 years. The earliest archaeological evidence in Australia of the use of coastal resources by Aboriginal people was recently found on the Cape Range Peninsula. This evidence has been radio-carbon dated at around 32,000 years. Middens (mounds of shells and other refuse) are found along the present coastline between Mangrove Bay and Yardie Creek and around Coral Bay, and there are rock shelters in the western foothills of Cape Range (near Mandu Mandu Creek, Pilgonamen Creek and Yardie Creek). Recent excavations of these sites have revealed extensive use of the peninsula's western coast by Aboriginal people between 32,000 to 400 years ago.

Evidence from the Mandu Mandu Creek rock shelter, however, indicates that human occupation of the site was intermittent. This rock shelter was possibly abandoned around 20,000 years ago during the glacial period, which resulted in extremely arid conditions and a drop in sea level of about 150 metres. It is likely that Cape Range inhabitants followed the shoreline, which retreated west, to between 10 and 12 kilometres from the present day shoreline.

At the end of the glacial period, sea levels rose again until they reached their present position, just over one kilometre from the foothills of Cape Range. This occurred from about 7000 to 3000 years ago and corresponds with evidence of increased use of the rock shelters.

Marine shells (especially balers, cone shells, mudwhelks, turban shells and topshells), fish (including parrotfish, tuskfish, bream, rockcod and rays), crabs, sea urchins, turtles, turtle eggs and dugongs were found in the various deposits. Remains of emu eggshells, kangaroos, bandicoots and other small mammals were also found.

Midden sites along the current shoreline provide evidence that there was a much more diverse intertidal environment between 7000 and 3000 years ago. Midden remains contain many species characteristic of mangrove habitats, indicating that

Left: *The lighthouse at Point Cloates.*
*Photo - Patrick Baker*
Right: *Unloading bales of wool from the jetty at Mauds Landing.*
*Photo - Courtesy of Rick French*

mangroves were much more extensive along the west coast then. Today, the only remaining remnant of mangrove vegetation between Exmouth Gulf and the Gascoyne River is at Mangrove Bay.

The traditional inhabitants of the area were the Jinigudjira, but they had disappeared from the Cape by the time the first pastoralists arrived. It is not known what caused their disappearance. It is possible that they were badly affected by diseases (such as smallpox) introduced by early European visitors.

# European history

The exploitation of the Exmouth Peninsula as a pastoral area began in the 1880s. Julius Brockman opened up Minilya Station and essentially took up the whole peninsula from Minilya north right up to North West Cape. Gradually the peninsula was divided up into the pastoral leases which exist now, and the early pioneers such as the French brothers, Matherson, the Le Froys and Carters, developed Ningaloo, Cardabia, Yardie Creek and Warroora, which are the main pastoral stations along the Ningaloo Reef.

The early communications in the area were largely by sea and the jetty at Mauds Landing (near what is today Coral Bay) was constructed in 1896-97. It remained the only port between Carnarvon and Onslow until the construction of the Norwest Cape installation at Exmouth in 1963. The jetty was quite a comprehensive structure extending 450 metres out to sea, with a 30 metre long and six metre wide T-head at the end. A 610 millimetre gauge tramway, a well and a large woolshed were also built, and the port served as a shipping point for wool, sheep and cattle up until the late 1930s. The last shipments were made from this jetty in about 1946.

However, the peninsula continued to be sparsely populated. The pastoral stations averaged 250,000 hectares in size, each operated by four to five people. The only road access was along the coast from Carnarvon via the Blowholes, through Quobba and Gnarloo stations up to Ningaloo. From here, the track swung inland through Bullara and Giralia to the North West Coastal Highway. This sandy track was often blocked by drifting sand, particularly at Gnarloo and Bullara, and was only travelled by the mail truck, station people and the most adventurous tourists. The coastal route further north was blocked by Yardie Creek, which even today is only passable by four-wheel-drive vehicles.

During the Second World War, an RAAF station was established at Learmonth, but this was primarily supplied by sea. The only land communication was via the Giralia Track from the North West Coastal Highway.

By the early 1950s, oil exploration company WAPET was starting to extend its interests into the area. At first it operated from the old RAAF landing area at Learmonth and spread its exploration teams from there, first into Cape Range and then it put a road through from Learmonth down to link up with Warroora. The main Exmouth/Minilya road was not put in until 1962, when the US Naval Wireless Communication Station was established at Exmouth and the town of Exmouth grew around it. However, the rough gravel track was not sealed until 1981. Once this road went in, tourism began to follow, but it was still very much a camping, four-wheel-drive exercise, mainly attracting fishermen with small boats. Exmouth was thus established as the northern gateway to the Ningaloo Reef, but it was still a 100 kilometre drive along a rough track around the tip of the North West Cape to reach Tantabiddy.

The Coral Bay Hotel and Caravan Park was opened in 1969. This quickly went bankrupt and it was not until 1980, with further development, that Coral Bay became established as the southern gateway to the reef.

# Fishing pressures on the reef

As early as 1792, American whalers were operating off the North West coast. At first they were mainly interested in sperm whales, but by the 1830s they had begun to understand the pattern of humpback whale migration (see p. 96-99). In 1870, 14 US whalers were operating off the North West coast. In 1913 a shore-based station opened up at Norwegian Bay, which operated for about four years, with three catcher boats bringing in up to four whales a day. This intensive fishing depleted the whale stock and the station closed down. It opened again in 1930 for a short time, and was finally reopened in 1951, using the original machinery which had been preserved by filling all cylinders and pipes with whale oil. The catchers operated out of Norwegian Bay until 1955, then transferred to Carnarvon. Whaling stocks were being depleted and catches fell from 1000 per year in the mid-1950s to only 87 in 1963, when whaling ceased.

The other major industry on the reef in the 1960s was turtle catching. Two licenses were granted, one to the mother ship *Tringa*, to operate south of Point Cloates, and the other to the *East Winds*, which operated north of the Point. Each mother ship operated four chaser boats. The turtles were chased in the shallow lagoon waters until they came up for air and were then harpooned. Only turtles over 45 kilograms could be taken, but catch rates of 90 to 100 turtles a day were achieved. Turtle fishing was banned in 1972, but the turtle population had been severely reduced and is only just starting to recover.

Rock lobster fishing in the area was limited to only two licenses. No pots were allowed, and rock lobsters could only be caught by diving for them. Only one license remains and this will lapse when the holder retires. Similarly, wetline fishing was not heavily commercially exploited, largely due to poor communications, and fish stocks did not come under pressure until increased tourism in the 1980s.

# Boom in tourism

The unique environment of the Ningaloo Marine Park and the North West Cape, the interest generated following the declaration of the marine park in 1987, and the facilities provided in the resort towns of Exmouth and Coral Bay have brought about a boom in tourism to the region.

From almost no visitors in 1980, the number of visitors to Exmouth has jumped to 49,000 visitor trips (331,000 visitor nights) in 1995 and 62,000 visitor trips (388,000 visitor nights) in 1996. Similarly, tourists to Coral Bay made 37,394 visitor trips (168,351 visitor nights) in 1995 and 37,417 visitor trips in 1996 (166,612 visitor nights). Many of these visitors are from overseas and interstate, and from March to June each year visitors from all around the world converge on Ningaloo for the experience of a lifetime - diving with the awesome whale shark, the world's biggest species of fish. The growth in tourism looks set to grow even further in the future.

# Sponges:
# simple but surprising

*Sponges are the simplest of all animals. They have no internal organs, appear motionless, and generally grow on underwater surfaces. It was only recently discovered that sponges actively pump water through their bodies to filter food. They are highly efficient filter feeders, and were a dominant form of life in our oceans 450 million years ago.*

Sponges have an outer layer of cells that are covered with tiny pores, or holes. The name of their phylum, Porifera, means 'pore-bearers'. These pores lead to an inner network of canals bordered by internal layers of cells. In most species of sponges, the internal skeleton contains slivers of silica, or spicules. The spicules vary in size and shape, but many are needle-like rods with pointed ends that can severely irritate the skin. It would therefore be unwise to use every sponge you find for your bathroom activities. Soft bath sponges come from a group of sponges that only contain a soft substance called spongin and lack spicules.

## Filter feeders

Sponges feed by passing water through their internal network of canals. The cells that line the canals are equipped with microscopic, hair-like projections called cilia. These create a current to move water through the canals. Plankton and other food particles are strained out and digested. Filtered water and wastes are expelled either through larger openings scattered among the pores, or through an open end of the sponge.

An average sponge filters its own volume of water every 10 to 12 seconds, so even a small sponge can filter hundreds of litres of water a day. In this way, sponges play an important role in filtering bacteria and organic particles from the water.

## Shape and habitat

Individual sponges of the same species may vary in colour and shape, depending on environmental conditions and where they are found. As a result, it is difficult to

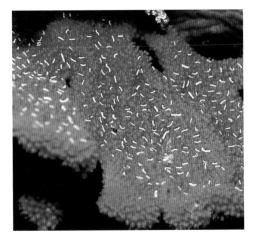

Left: *Sponges come in all shapes, colours and sizes.*
Right: *Tiny white worms coat the surface of this sponge.*
*Photos - Ann Storrie*

identify sponges from photographs, and microscopic examination of the skeleton (the spicules and spongin) is usually required.

Water currents seem to have the greatest effect on sponges. In areas that experience strong water movement, sponges may take an encrusting form. This means that they form a thin layer of cells, often only a few millimetres thick, that grows over underwater surfaces, or on top of other invertebrates. Some corals, for instance, are sometimes coated with an encrusting sponge that gives its host an attractive colour.

Some sponges may grow into huge, barrel-shaped specimens large enough to contain a diver. Others tower above the reef like pillars or chimneys. Divers have given common names to sponges which relate to their shape. Hence you have barrel sponges, hand and finger sponges, cup sponges and ball sponges, among others.

## Sex and the single sponge

If a sponge is mashed, passed through a fine sieve, and the cells placed together in a container, they can regroup to form a new sponge, or several small sponges. It is not known what mechanisms regulate the growth of a sponge, or how they adapt their shape to the environmental conditions.

Sponges can reproduce asexually by simply producing a tiny ball, or bud, of sponge that breaks off and forms a new adult. Sometimes, sponges will be covered in tiny buds, ready to break away from their parents.

Sponges can also reproduce sexually and may be male, female or hermaphrodite. Hermaphrodites are individuals that can produce both sperm and eggs. To avoid self-fertilisation, some species produce only one type of reproductive cell at a time. Sponges reproduce sexually at the most favourable time of year for survival of the young. Sperm and eggs are liberated into the water, where fertilisation takes place, leading to the formation of a free-swimming, or crawling, larva. Sponges can also be brooders, where sperm is released, fertilisation is internal, eggs and embryos are incubated and a larva released. The larva may survive for several days, then settles onto the bottom to grow into an adult.

*Sponges are simple animals with tiny pores, or holes that lead to an inner network of canals.*
*Photo - Ann Storrie*

*Sponges can reproduce by budding. This ball sponge is producing buds that are tiny replicas of itself. The buds will float in the current until they land on the reef some distance away. Photo - Ann Storrie*

## Sponging off others

Although sponges are extremely efficient filter feeders, some waters do not have enough nutrients to sustain large populations. While this is often true on coral reefs, many sponges have overcome this problem by taking microscopic blue-green algae (cyanobacteria) into their tissues. The algae, through photosynthesis using sunlight, produce energy-rich sugar compounds, which leak into the sponge tissue. In some species of sponges, the algae supplies most of the sponge's nutritional needs. A similar relationship with algae also often occurs with corals, molluscs and ascidians.

Many other animals live in a close relationship with sponges. Some species of sea cucumbers and tiny tubeworms live on sponges and feed on particles or chemicals that coat the surface of the sponge. Feather stars (crinoids) often perch on top of large sponges to gain access to the current and passing plankton. The numerous canals within the sponge provide hiding places for many crabs, shrimps and worms. Some animals, such as nudibranchs, even associate with sponges because the unpleasant taste of many sponges repels predators.

You can find hundreds of species of sponges in the Ningaloo Marine Park, especially around Bundegi Reef in Exmouth Gulf. Although they may seem uninteresting members of the reef community, close observation of their design, and of the animals living on or in them, could give you an enlightened view of the humble sponge.

# Creative corals & their cousins

*At first glance, corals, anemones, hydroids and jellyfish appear to be a miscellaneous collection, but they are all grouped together in one large phylum, the Cnidaria (pronounced ny-dare-ea). Two characteristics link these animals together: they all possess stinging cells called cnidoblasts and they all have a similar basic body plan. There are more than 9000 species in the Indo-Pacific region.*

This phylum is divided into four separate classes. They are:
1. Hard corals, soft corals, and their relatives (Class Anthozoa)
2. Hydroids, fire corals, Portuguese man o'war (Class Hydrozoa)
3. Jellyfish (Class Scyphozoa)
4. Box jellyfish (Class Cubozoa)

## Stinging cells

The stinging cells (cnidoblasts) are found on the tentacles, and are so small that they are generally not visible to the naked eye. However, in some animals, such as the hard coral *Tubastrea*, groups of stinging cells are visible on the tentacles as small raised dots. The cnidoblast contains a vesicle (nematocyst) which encloses a harpoon-like stinging mechanism. When undischarged, the stinging mechanism lies coiled up like a spring. The Portuguese man o'war can cause intense pain to people unfortunate enough to swim into its long tentacles. Each tentacle is armed with thousands of stinging cells, which together can inflict a large quantity of venom. At the other end of the scale is the cherry anemone (*Actinia tenebrosa*) common in intertidal areas. If you touch the tentacles with your fingers, they feel sticky. This sensation is due to the stinging cells attaching to your skin, but the venom cannot penetrate the tough skin, so no pain is inflicted.

## Body plan

All Cnidaria have a simple cup-shaped body with tentacles around the rim, and a central opening that acts as both a mouth and an anus. There are two body

Left: *Tree coral (*Dendronephthya *sp.)*
Photo - Paul Jelley
Right: *Close-up of* Goniopora *sp.*
Photo - Gerhard Sauracker

*These large, yellow polyps (Tubastrea sp.) inhabit ledges and caves. Photo - Peter and Margy Nicholas*

forms based on this theme. The sedentary (attached) polyp (such as a coral polyp or anemone) and the free-swimming medusa (like jellyfish). The medusa is like an upside down polyp, but without any base for attachment.

Some classes have both body forms in their development. In jellyfish the polyp is small and the main phase of the life cycle is spent as a free-swimming medusa. Hydroids have a small medusa, which in turn produces eggs that develop into sedentary polyps. In corals, however, only sedentary polyps exist without a medusa phase.

# Hard corals, soft corals and their cousins

True (hard) corals are in the Class Anthozoa, which also includes soft corals, black corals, sea anemones and zoanthids. The theme linking these animals together is the fact that none of them have a free-living medusa in their life cycle, only the sedentary polyp stage.

This class is further divided into four subclasses:

1) The Hexacorallia (Zoantharia) include the hard corals, sea anemones and zoanthids. Tentacles are usually in multiples of six.
2) The Octocorallia (Alcyonaria) include soft corals, gorgonians, sea whips and sea pens. Members of this subclass have tentacles which are always eight in number and feathery.
3) The Antipatharia include the black or thorny corals. The polyps have simple, unbranched tentacles.
4) The Cerianthuria include the tube anemones. These are large, solitary polyps with two whorls of slender tentacles.

## Hard corals

The true hard corals, or stony corals, are distinguished by having a hard skeleton and tentacles usually arranged in groups of six, or multiples of six. Hard corals are responsible for building spectacular coral reefs, the largest structures built by living animals. The coral polyps have skeletons of limestone (calcium carbonate). With successive generations, further calcium carbonate is deposited on the old skeletons and so the colony grows in size. Very large colonies, many hundreds of years old, can develop in some of the slow-growing species, such as large bommies of massive corals (*Porites*). A huge colony lives in the middle of Coral Bay, and is appropriately named Ayers Rock.

Many hard coral polyps have tiny, single-celled algae, called zooxanthellae, inhabiting their tissues. Both the polyp and the algae benefit from this association. The polyp gains nutrients (organic carbon) which leak out of the algae, and the algae have a safe place to live. Because the algae can photosynthesise (obtain energy using sunlight), coral can grow faster in light than in darkness. This factor allows coral to keep ahead of erosion (by wave action and borers) in its growth rate. Corals that contain these algae are called hermatypic, or reef-building corals, and most are colonial. An exception is the mushroom coral (*Fungia*).

Some hard corals lack zooxanthellae in their tissues. These are known as ahermatypic corals and do not form reefs. They do not depend on light (because they lack the algae) and can therefore grow at greater depths than reef-building corals. Less than one third of these corals are colonial, and those that are do not form such large colonies as the hermatypic corals eg *Tubastrea* and *Dendrophyllia*. Many of the non reef-building corals are small, solitary cave dwellers.

## Feeding

Reef-building corals derive up to 98 per cent of their nutrients from the symbiotic algae. The rest of their food is derived from plankton captured with the tentacles. Some plankton migrate vertically on a 24 hour time frame and may only enter shallow water at night. Other plankton are carried in ocean currents. The pattern of food availability explains why different species of corals extend and retract their polyps at varying times of the day and night.

Non reef-building corals are wholly carnivorous and feed on a range of animals including plankton, worms and fish.

## Reproduction and growth

Corals are versatile in that they can reproduce both asexually and sexually. In asexual reproduction, coral polyps bud off from each other as the colony grows. There is no limit to the number of new polyps produced, and colonies could theoretically grow to huge dimensions. The limiting factors on colony size varies for different species, for instance, the fast-growing staghorn corals are more susceptible to wave action, borers and their own weight as they increase in size, whereas the slower-growing, more solid massive (*Porites*) corals can withstand these factors better and may grow to several metres in height and diameter over hundreds of years.

*A small colony of staghorn coral* (Acropora *sp.*) *in which the polyps are visible. Photo - Sue Morrison*

*A brain coral* (Platygyra daedalea). *Photo - Sue Morrison*

Corals can also reproduce asexually when clumps of polyps break off (perhaps due to wave action) and land in a suitable spot to grow. Some corals can asexually produce larvae which are then dispersed in the ocean currents.

During sexual reproduction, eggs and sperm are released and unite to form planulae larvae. Most coral polyps have both male and female gonads, while others have separate male and female colonies, such as *Goniopora*. Some species may fertilise internally. In internal fertilisation the sperm fertilises the egg within the polyp.

In the majority of species, however, fertilisation is external. For this to be successful, with wave action, currents and predators to disrupt proceedings, a synchronised mechanism has evolved. Dramatic mass coral spawning occurs only on a few nights of the year! This has been extensively studied in the last 15 years and takes place at different times in different locations. In Ningaloo Marine Park mass coral spawning occurs in early autumn (March to April), whereas in the Great Barrier Reef it occurs in late spring. Just after dark, eggs and sperm are released into the water in such huge numbers that the water turns cloudy.

This mass coral spawning is a spectacular event at Ningaloo Marine Park, with many other invertebrates also reproducing at the same time. This results in a very rich collection of larvae in the plankton, which in turn attracts many plankton feeders, including the massive whale sharks. Although water clarity is not optimum at this time of year, it is a great time to visit because of the incredible wealth of marine life concentrated in the area.

## Competition for space

When different coral species grow in close proximity to each other, there is competition for space and light. Faster growing corals with fine branches, such as staghorn corals (*Acropora* spp.), can easily out-compete encrusting, slower-growing species. In the long run, however, the encrusting colony could live longer because it is better able to withstand destructive forces. Many factors can interact and affect the survival of coral colonies.

Colonies which come into close contact can display aggression. In some species the polyps can extend their tentacles and wave them towards the competitor and even sting them. These battle grounds can often be seen as dead, bare patches around the margins of adjacent colonies. It can even result in one colony overgrowing and killing the entire competing colony.

## Predators

Besides competition from other corals, there is the problem of coral predators. These include the well known crown-of-thorns starfish (*Acanthaster planci*). It is only found in Ningaloo Marine Park in very low numbers, and does not pose a major threat to coral populations in this region. It is still not known what causes huge fluctuations in starfish populations on the Great Barrier Reef, but it is likely that they are natural events, exacerbated to some extent by human activities.

Another well-studied predator of corals is a small gastropod mollusc (*Drupella cornus*). It has been observed in large numbers in Ningaloo Marine Park and has killed large patches of coral where it has been feeding on the polyps (see p. 43-44).

Less easy to see are marine borers such as worms, molluscs and sponges. Borers can make numerous holes in coral colonies, but generally tend to reach a balance with corals and are not an important threat.

Surprisingly, fish are great predators on coral. In some areas they eat about one third of the annual growth of coral. Parrotfish, in particular, can often be seen (and heard) crunching on coral colonies. They leave tell-tale white tooth marks on the coral. This is the natural diet for these fish, and corals have evolved to survive such attacks.

## Other damage

The biggest threat to the reef is, ironically, coral spawning. If coral spawn dies and decomposes, it absorbs large quantities of oxygen from the water. If a westerly wind prevails for two or three days during the spawning period, the spawn is pushed into the bays and lagoons, deoxygenating the water and killing corals, territorial fish and other animals. The most recent major example of this occurred in the Coral Bay area in 1989, when more than 50 per cent of some fish species were killed, along with 25 per cent of the coral. Dead fish, eels, crabs and shells littered the beaches for weeks. This tends to happen each year on a small scale at the north end of Coral Bay, where the prevailing southerly and south-westerly winds push spawn under the curve of Point Maud. The corals and fish in this area are much reduced compared to the open water areas of the bay.

Corals are subject to many other forms of physical damage, both natural and man-made. Cyclones can break up large areas of coral, particularly in shallow waters. These are natural events from which corals are able to recover. Of greater concern is man-made damage, such as boat anchorages, dynamiting reefs for boat channels and fishing, and developments on reef edges. Such damage, combined with a barrage of pollutants, poses a great threat to many of our extensive coral reefs. It is sobering to think that reefs such as Ningaloo have taken thousands of years to develop, but in less than 100 years, human activities have had a serious detrimental effect on them. Corals are a

Above: *This* Pocillopora *sp., like other members of the genus, has small, wart-like nodules on the branches. Photo - Sue Morrison*
Below: *An exceptionally large colony of cabbage coral (*Turbinaria *sp.). Photo - Gerhard Saueracker*

major part of the marine ecosystem and must be given full protection to ensure the future survival of our oceans. We are fortunate that human activities have had a minimal impact on Ningaloo Reef so far. We must ensure that it stays that way.

## Hard corals in Ningaloo Marine Park

Representatives of all 15 families of reef-building corals found in Australia have been recorded in Ningaloo Marine Park. Some are described here. Most corals are hard to identify to species level underwater, or from photographs, because it is often necessary to examine the polyps and skeleton at a microscopic level. The same coral species can vary in colour and shape with depth and location on the reef, further adding to the problems of identification. Many examples cited here, therefore, only include the genus.

**Family Acroporidae**
The Acroporidae, often known as staghorn and plate corals, are the major building blocks of coral reefs. They are numerous in the clear waters of upper reef slopes. They include a great variety of growth forms, including the branched staghorn forms (*Acropora robusta*, *Acropora florida*), flat plates (*Acropora hyacinthus*) and encrusting forms (*Montipora* spp.)

**Family Faviidae**
The Faviidae have more genera than any other coral families and all are reef builders. They include brain corals (such as *Platygyra* spp.) and honeycomb corals (*Goniastrea* spp.), which grow in rounded lumps (massive form) or encrusting forms. Also common are *Favia* spp. and *Favites* spp., which are usually massive, and *Echinopora* spp., which can have varied growth forms.

**Family Pocilloporidae**
The family Pocilloporidae are often found on upper reef slopes in exposed conditions. The genus *Pocillopora* is most easily recognised because of the small lumps (verrucae) over the surface of the branches, such as in *Pocillopora verrucosa* and *P. eydouxi*, but they are absent in *P. damicornis*. *Seriatopora* is also easy to recognise from the more slender branches, such as in *S. hystrix*.

**Family Poritidae**
The family Poritidae can form extremely large massive colonies up to several hundred years old, such as *Porites* spp. The very small polyps give the colonies a smooth appearance from a distance. A stunning example is 'Ayers Rock', located in the middle of Bill's Bay (Coral Bay), which is approximately seven metres in diameter and three metres high. In contrast, the genus *Goniopora* is quite different in appearance, having large, fleshy polyps with 24 tentacles. Also similar is the genus *Alveopora*, in which the polyps have only 12 tentacles.

**Family Fungiidae**
The Fungiidae are mostly solitary, free-living corals (not attached to underwater surfaces). Some species are readily recognised, such as mushroom corals (*Fungia* spp.) and slipper corals (*Herpolitha* spp. and *Polyphyllia* spp.), which have some of the largest individual polyps. A few species are capable of limited movement and can slowly move away if covered in sand.

**Family Dendrophylliidae**
The Family Dendrophylliidae contains both reef-building and non reef-building genera. The most familiar reef builders are cabbage corals (*Turbinaria* spp.), which have plates that form characteristic large whorls. Several non reef-building genera are frequently

Clockwise from top left: Symphyllia *sp. in the Family Mussidea (Photo - Paul Jelley);* Porites lichen *in the Family Poritidae (Photo - Gerhard Saueracker);* Fungia *sp. in the Family Fungiidae (Photo - Vivien Matson-Larkin); the bubble coral* Euphyllia divisa *in the Family Caryophyllidae (Photo - Ann Storrie);* Galaxea *sp. in the Family Oculinidae (Photo - Sue Morrison); and* Merulina ampliata *in the Family Merulinidae (Photo - Sue Morrison).*

seen by divers on coral reefs in caves and ledges. These include *Tubastrea* spp. and *Dondrophyllia* spp., which have large bright yellow, orange or olive green polyps.

**Family Mussidae**
Species in this widespread family have heavily constructed skeletons with thick, fleshy colourful polyps. Two genera (*Lobophyllia* and *Symphyllia*) have very large corallites and valleys. The colonies tend to be flat-topped or dome-shaped.

**Family Caryophyllidae**
The Caryophyllidae are only found in small numbers, but are easily recognised. They are known as the bubble corals (*Euphyllia* sp.) and grape corals (*Plerogyra* sp).

**Family Merulinidae**
Colonies of *Merulina* spp. can have a combination of flat plates and small branches. They are characterised by small valleys which radiate out from the centre of the colony on the flat plates, but are contorted on the branches.

**Family Oculinidae**
Only one genus, *Galaxea*, is found at Ningaloo, where it occurs in most habitats. The other genera in this family are non reef-building and most live in deep waters.

## Sea anemones

Sea anemones are conspicuous, sometimes brightly coloured, individual polyps. They have no skeleton and are attached at their base to rocks or other firm underwater surfaces (sometimes to hermit crab shells!). Some species can grow to huge proportions, such as *Heteractis magnifica*, while the bulb-tentacle sea anemone (*Entacmaea quadricolor*), in which anemonefish often live, appears to be a huge individual, but is usually a field of anemones clustered together. Sea anemones have the ability to creep slowly with the aid of their muscular 'foot'. They feed on a variety of animals including worms, crustaceans and fish, which they trap in their tentacles. Many species are harmless to people, but some can cause painful stings.

## Zoanthids

Zoanthids look very similar to sea anemones, but are usually colonial, being joined at the base. They often have a sausage-shaped body a few centimetres long (visible when the tentacles are retracted) and a rim of short tentacles around the mouth. One genus (*Palythoa*) is highly toxic if ingested, but does not sting.

*This* Montipora *sp., in the Family Acroporidae, has plates which grow in whorls. Photo - Sue Morrison*

*Gorgonians often grow in a single plane with multiple branches. Photo - Paul Jelley*

## Soft corals

Soft corals do not possess a solid skeleton like the hard corals, but instead have small, calcareous structures called sclerites embedded in their tissue. These sclerites, along with water pressure, support the main body of the colony. The elaborate shape of the microscopic sclerites is important in identifying different species. Thus, it is often difficult to positively identify soft coral species underwater.

Soft corals all have some degree of flexibility. Some soft corals feel leathery or rubbery, such as *Sinularia* and *Sarcophyton*, while others are prickly, such as *Dendronephthya*. In the latter genus, small, elongated sclerites can be seen on the outer surface of the stem walls of the colony, and large, pointy sclerites protrude between the soft polyps.

Many soft corals are drab in colour, including the reef-top *Lobophytum*, *Sarcophyton* and *Sinularia*. Other species, at deeper levels, are some of the most colourful animals on the reef. The *Nephtheids*, for example, can be bright pinks, yellows, oranges or reds.

## Gorgonians and sea whips

Gorgonians (sea fans) and sea whips are plant-like in shape. Sea fans usually grow in a flat fan-shape with multiple branches, each bearing numerous, small polyps. Others grow in a more three-dimensional pattern. Like soft corals, they have sclerites in their tissues, but they also have a horn-like material called gorgonin, which makes them fairly rigid.

Some gorgonians grow to huge sizes, over a metre in diameter, particularly where there are strong currents, and hence a plentiful supply of food. They are often colourful, with orange, yellow or red surface tissue and contrasting white polyps.

Sea whips are slender, long and unbranched, with polyps distributed along the surface. The stem contains horny material which gives it support. Sea whips tend to be found in deeper waters, on the outside of the reef, for example off Tantabiddy.

*The yellow or white surface tissue disguises the black skeleton of black coral* (Antipathes *sp.*). *Photo - Sue Morrison*

## Blue coral

Blue coral (*Heliopora coerulea*) is the only species in the Family Helioporidae. It is found on the reef flats and upper reef slopes. The colonies can be branched, columnar, or plate-like. Though blue coral is a reef-building, colonial species, it is not a true hard coral. There are eight tentacles on each polyp. Despite its common name, blue coral is externally greenish-grey, with white polyps. The internal part of the skeleton is blue, but this is only visible if the colony is broken.

## Sea pens

Sea pens have a central, unbranched main stem that bears the polyps. The fringed tentacles on the polyps give the colony the appearance of a feather writing quill, hence the name 'sea pen'. At the base of the main stem, a bulbous stalk holds the colony in the sediment. The colony is supported by water (the stalk has four canals which expand when filled with water), but can retract into the sediment if water is expelled from the canals.

Some very small, thin species are found in the Ningaloo lagoon. However, sea pens are not frequently seen when diving because they tend to be found in areas of silty sand, and many are nocturnal and only emerge after dark. If you are fortunate enough to find a sea pen at night, try giving it a gentle tap because it will provide you with a beautiful light show when it phosphoresces (turn your torch down too!).

## Black corals

Black or thorny corals have an internal thorny skeleton composed of a strong, dark protein called horn. This black skeleton is highly prized for the manufacture of black coral jewellery, although nowadays the aim is to conserve these beautiful, slow-growing colonies. In live black coral colonies, the black skeleton is hidden by the white or yellow living surface tissue.

The polyps have an unusual arrangement of six tentacles that cannot be retracted. The colonies can grow in a bushy form or in long, thin, coiled whips. Black corals tend to grow in deeper waters, particularly on vertical walls.

## Tube anemones

Tube anemones (cerianthids) look similar to sea anemones, but lack a basal disc and have long, muscular bodies (up to 40 centimetres long in some species). The rim of the tube anemone bears an outer ring of slender, long tentacles and an inner ring of shorter ones. They build mucus tubes in the soft sediment around their bases, into which they can rapidly retract if disturbed.

# Hydroids, Portuguese man o'wars and fire corals

The Class Hydrozoa includes hydroids (such as sea ferns and fire weed), Portuguese man o'wars (blue bottles) and fire corals. Hydrozoa are only distantly related to true corals, but have several features in common with jellyfish. Individual polyps can perform specific functions including feeding, reproduction and defence. The defence polyps are so specialised that they lack a mouth and are covered in a dense battery of stinging cells. Not surprisingly, many of these animals are known for their ability to cause painful stings.

## Hydroids

Hydroids often look like finely-branched, feathery plants, hence the name sea ferns. These are in fact colonies of polyps. Each slender branch bears a row of minute polyps. Many colonies have a chitinous exoskeleton (outer skeleton). Two species of colonial hydroids found at Ningaloo can cause painful stings. These are *Aglaophaenia cupressina*, which is pale brown and up to 30 centimetres high, and the more conspicuous *Lytocarpus philippinus*, which is white and reaches 15 centimetres high. Many other attractive hydroid colonies are found on the reef, often smaller than these stinging varieties. Occasionally, hydroids consisting of a single large polyp, up to 5 centimetres high, from the genus *Ralpharia*, can be seen. Hydroids have two stages in their life cycle, a polyp stage which reproduces by budding and branching, and a medusa stage which reproduces sexually.

## Portuguese man o'war

The Portuguese man o'war (*Physalia physalis*), or blue bottle, looks like a jellyfish but is in fact a colony. It is composed of a gas-filled float (up to 15 centimetres long) attached to a colony of specialised polyps and feeding tentacles. The largest tentacle can extend up to 10 metres long and is covered with thousands of stinging cells. These animals are most commonly seen when washed ashore by strong winds. When stranded on the beach, the attractive blue float is the most conspicuous part and the tentacles and polyps are usually contracted and shrivelled up. Even when dead these can often cause a painful rash, so do not touch them if you find them washed up on the beach.

## Hydrozoan corals

Fire coral looks more like a hard coral than a hydroid, because it has a hard, calcareous skeleton. The skeleton has a pattern of tiny holes for feeding polyps, surrounded by a circle of even smaller pores for stinging polyps. There is also a medusa stage in the life cycle, unlike true corals. A fire coral (*Millepora platyphylla*) often seen on the reef flats and lagoon reefs in Ningaloo Marine Park consists of solid, smooth, yellowish-brown plates, with paler yellow edges. There is also a multi-branched species, which often

*Tube anemones are more closely related to black corals than anemones.*
*Photo - Sue Morrison*

*Saucer jellyfish* (Aurelia aurita) *may appear in huge congregations in the Ningaloo Marine Park. This is not a stinging species. Photo - Paul Jelley*

forms thickets. Other species of non-stinging hydrocorals have a finer, branched structure and are found in caves and on vertical walls. They are usually pink or purple.

## Jellyfish and box jellyfish

The Class Scyphozoa contains the jellyfish, and Class Cubozoa, the box jellyfish. These animals have a conspicuous medusa and a small polyp stage in their life cycle.

Jellyfish are weak swimmers and float in ocean currents. They feed on a range of organisms from plankton to crustaceans and fish. Some species are harmless to people, such as the saucer jelly (*Aurelia aurita*), but others, such as the mauve stinger (*Pelagia noctiluca*) and hairy stinger (*Cyanea mjobergi*), can deliver painful stings.

Box jellyfish are distinguished from other jellyfish by their box-shaped medusa, and the arrangement of one or more tentacles on each of the four 'corners'. Box jellyfish are difficult to see, as the animal is often colourless with a small medusa and long, trailing tentacles. Sometimes they are spotted from their shadows on the sand.

The most venomous species is the multi-tentacled sea wasp (*Chironex fleckeri*). This species usually occurs further north than the Ningaloo Marine Park. No fatalities from sea wasp stings have been recorded in the north-west of Australia. However, severe stings requiring hospitalisation in the Ningaloo-Exmouth area have been caused by a very large four-tentacled species of *Tamoya*. A small warty species, the Irukandji box jellyfish, causes severe general symptoms and can be expected anywhere in the north-west. Other less venomous species may be encountered in the plankton. For example, jimble (*Carybdea rastoni*) is found all around the Australian coastline.

# A wonderland of worms

*The word 'worm' conjures up images of long, slimy beasts. Earthworms, roundworms and tapeworms may be long and slimy, but there are thousands of species of marine worms that are nothing like their cousins. Many are creatures of outstanding beauty and amazing diversity in structure and form.*

All coral reefs are teeming with worms. A study on Heron Island in the Great Barrier Reef showed 1441 worms from 103 species living in, and on, a three kilogram coral head. This was about two thirds of the total fauna population on that piece of coral. If anyone studied a piece of coral from Ningaloo, the statistics would probably be similar.

Worms range from microscopic organisms to several centimetres long. Some burrow into coral and construct tubes to house their soft bodies. Other species live totally exposed on the surface of corals, rocks or sand, while some species are free-swimming and live among plankton. They are all important parts of the ecosystem of a coral reef.

## Christmas tree worms and other polychaete worms

Polychaete worms have elongated, segmented bodies, with a mouth at one end and an anus at the other. Their digestive, circulatory and nervous systems are well developed. The best known are probably the colourful Christmas tree worms (*Spirobranchus giganteus*) that live in tubes, usually within hard corals. Divers do not see the body of these worms, just the feather-like feeding tentacles that protrude from their tube. The tentacles trap plankton, which is moved down grooves to the animal's mouth. A chalky plug or plate may also be seen just beside the tentacles. This is like a door that plugs the top of the tube when the worm contracts its tentacles inside.

The tentacles are very sensitive to light and pressure. As underwater photographers know, the slightest movement, or shadow, can result in a photograph of the top of a hollow tube, instead of the colourful display of feathery tentacles. The tentacles are withdrawn very quickly, but if you are patient and still, the animal may slowly unravel its tentacles again as you watch.

Left: *Christmas tree worm.*
Right: *Fan worm.*
*Photos - Ann Storrie*

Unlike many other worms, which are hermaphrodites, most polychaete worms have separate sexes. Eggs and sperm from different Christmas tree worms are released into the water at the same time. The resulting larvae settle onto the reef two to three weeks after fertilisation. They secrete a tube that kills the underlying coral polyps, but new coral growth quickly forms around the tube. As the coral continues to grow, the worms must also extend their tubes to keep pace with the surface layer of coral.

Some polychaete worms live on sponges. They build white, neatly constructed tubes that only measure a few millimetres long. They space themselves evenly over the surface of the sponge, at a distance equalling the length of their tentacles. If you find a sponge with tiny white blobs on it, take a closer look. You may be able to discern the tubes and, at their ends, two fine tentacles waving across the surface of the sponge. If you approach too closely the tentacles will disappear.

There are many other polychaete worms, some of which are not so innocuous. Fire worms live under rocks and within coral. Salmon pink fire worms (*Eurythoe complanata*) are quite colourful, and appear soft and inoffensive. Their bristles, however, are hollow and contain venom that can cause considerable irritation if stuck into fingers.

Another worm that is covered with bristles is the sea mouse (*Aphrodite australis*). This tiny, stout, mouse-shaped worm buries itself in sand and emerges at night to feed. Its fine bristles resemble fur but will, however, pierce the skin and cause a nettle-like sting and irritation that can last for hours. The 'mice' are none-the-less interesting creatures. Look for small brown mounds in the sand if night diving in Coral Bay.

## Fabulous flatworms

Luckily, not all marine flatworms look or live like their close relatives, tapeworms and liver flukes, which infest many fish and terrestrial animals. The flatworms seen by divers are generally colourful animals that are often mistaken for nudibranchs (sea slugs). Some even mimic the colours of nudibranchs as a form of defence against predators (see p. 44-48). They are, however, flatter and do not possess the feathery gills and tentacles of nudibranchs. They range in size from microscopic to about 15

*An acorn worm mound.*
*Photo - Ann Storrie*

*Flatworms are often mistaken for sea slugs or nudibranchs, but they are flatter than nudibranchs and do not have feathery gills or tentacles. Photo - Leslie Newman and Andrew Flowers*

centimetres long. Flatworms are often seen moving over various underwater surfaces, however far more are found under rocks and among coral rubble.

Like snails, flatworms secrete a film of mucus on which to move about, and are propelled by fine bristles that cover their underbody. They can also swim for short distances by undulating their body margins in a graceful motion.

Most flatworms are hermaphrodites. However, they do not self-fertilise. Theoretically, the worms try to insert their male reproductive organs into the female opening of the other. This is not always the case, and often each will puncture the other several times to inject sperm directly into the recipient's body cavity. Fortunately, flatworms can regenerate an entire new animal from a detached fragment, so their mating habits rarely prove fatal.

## Acorn worms

Have you ever passed over a coiled mass of tubules on the sandy sea floor and wondered what it was? If you stopped and poked it, it would disintegrate into grains of sand. That's because it is mainly sand. It has been deposited by an acorn worm (*Balanoglossus clavigerus*) that has excavated a U-shaped burrow beneath it. In a sense, the mounds are faeces, as the sand has been eaten and excreted by the acorn worm as it forms its burrow. The animal also extracts food particles from the sand, so the mounds are known as faecal castings. Within the body of an acorn worm are many gland cells that secrete mucus. As the worm burrows, it lays mucus along the walls of the tunnel to cement the sand particles together and prevent the burrow from collapsing. Although you may never see an acorn worm, acknowledge its creativity the next time you pass over a mound of its castings.

# Sea shells, sea slugs and other molluscs

*Molluscs form one of the largest divisions of the animal kingdom. Marine molluscs include gastropods, such as snail-like, spiral-shaped sea shells and sea slugs; bivalves such as oysters and clams; cephalopods such as cuttlefish, octopuses and squid; and some other groups, two of which are chitons and elephant-tusk shells.*

All molluscs have a soft, non-segmented body and a mantle, or fleshy membrane, which envelops the body, lines the shell and, in some groups, covers all or part of the shell's outer surface. The mantle contains special cells that secrete calcium carbonate, and is responsible for the manufacture and continuous repair of the shell. Most molluscs also have a muscular foot on which to move about. Even octopus arms were derived from this feature. Gills for respiration are usually present, and most molluscs have a radula, a tongue-like apparatus used for rasping fragments of food.

Since there are probably about 80,000 species of molluscs in the sea, some hundreds of which have been recorded from Ningaloo, we describe only a few of the most common and interesting groups in the marine park.

## Conserving sea shells

Shell collecting was probably one of our first hobbies. Who can resist collecting shells on a beach? Today, the science known as Malacology deals with the study of the ecology and natural history of living and extinct molluscs. It has led to a new awareness of shells as living animals. In Ningaloo Marine Park, molluscs are protected and no collecting is allowed. Even empty shells can provide homes for other animals, such as hermit crabs and small fish, and the breakdown of the shells contributes to the formation of sand.

## One-footed wonders

Gastropods are the most common sea shells. They usually have a single, basically coiled shell that protects the soft-bodied mollusc.

Left: *The Western Australian nudibranch* (Chromodoris westraliensis).
*Photo - Vivien Matson-Larkin*
Right: *The colourful mantle of a clam.*
*Photo - Ann Storrie*

## Cowries and their allies

The group of gastropods known as cowries has an interesting history. Cowries were traded for labour and goods throughout Asia, Africa and much of the Pacific. In parts of India, they were the sole currency for centuries. This was probably due to the cowry's striking colours, patterns, glossy texture and pleasing shape. The shells of these animals are still irresistible to many divers but, in these conservation-aware times, most people are content to admire them then leave them where they are. In the Ningaloo Marine Park, remember to observe and take photographs but do not remove them.

Most cowries live in tropical waters, though some are found in temperate seas. A mixture of both tropical and temperate forms is found at Ningaloo Reef. Although most people can easily recognise cowries, live specimens may be well camouflaged by the enveloping mantle. When the cowry is undisturbed, its fleshy mantle folds up over the shell from either side. The mantle is often mottled with similar colours to its habitat, and may be covered with pustules and small tentacles which also act as camouflage.

Ovulids are allies of the cowry family. They include spindle cowries, which feed on gorgonians and other corals. These shellfish nearly always assume the same colour as their prey and are often hard to find. One of the largest, the egg cowry (*Ovula ovum*), can grow more than 12 centimetres long. Its shell is pure white and an unblemished specimen is magnificent. The real beauty, however, is in its mantle which can be velvet black studded with white or yellow pustules. Egg cowries live along Ningaloo Reef and have been found feeding on soft corals in the shallows of Coral Bay.

*Egg cowries are often seen feeding on soft corals in Coral Bay. Photo - Ann Storrie*

Drupella cornus, *a small marine snail, consumes living coral, leaving the white, dead coral skeleton behind. Photo - Ann Storrie*

## Baler shells

Baler shells are giants among the gastropods and are the largest species in the volute family. A shell of the species *Melo amphora* (a tropical species seen at Ningaloo Marine Park which is distributed from Shark Bay to Queensland) has been measured at more than 50 centimetres long. Early Europeans recorded Aboriginal people bailing out their canoes with these huge shells. Hence, the corrupted name baler.

Balers are generally nocturnal animals that hunt for other molluscs on sandy bottoms or reefs. By day, they usually bury themselves in the sand. They are occasionally found in the sheltered waters of Coral Bay. If you are lucky, you may see one laying its eggs, which it attaches to rocks or seagrasses on the sea floor, during the day. Other smaller volute species are commonly found in the coral, on the intertidal reef areas and on sand along the coast.

## Cone shells

Cone shells are all carnivores and their radula has evolved into a series of hollow harpoons which can be filled with venom. A number of these are stored within a gland opening into the mouth and can be shot out like a dart, or held and plunged into the body of the prey. Depending on the species, cones prey on other molluscs, worms or fish. The venom of each species is specific to one type of prey. However, the venom of cone shells is dangerous to people, and that of fish-eating species may cause death. Many colourful and exquisitely patterned cones are common on ledges and in crevices within the marine park. Others may be coated with the horny outer shell layer or in coralline algae and are well-camouflaged, so it is wise to be careful where you place an ungloved hand. The dangerous geographer cone (*Conus geographus*) is found in Coral

Bay. This large cone, up to 12 centimetres long, is usually found in sandy pockets near the reef edge, or on the reef itself. It has caused several human deaths.

## Whelks

This group includes the *Drupella* species. *Drupella cornus*, a small marine snail that eats coral, is prevalent in Ningaloo Marine Park, and its feeding habits can be almost as devastating to the coral reef as those of the crown-of-thorns sea star have been elsewhere. The snail browses over the reef, consuming the living coral tissue and leaving a ghostly white skeleton. This can have great impact on the ecosystems of the reef. Seaweeds often grow over the coral skeleton, which then attracts populations of seaweed-eating animals. The dead coral may disintegrate and animals that rely on coral for food decrease in number, so the entire ecosystem can change.

Divers may find this snail quite insignificant. It is usually around three centimetres long and often congregates underneath the coral and beneath ledges during the day. Where severe outbreaks of *Drupella cornus* are occurring, however, several snails may be seen feeding on the coral and leaving a white skeleton behind them.

Although *Drupella cornus* is part of the natural reef fauna, populations of this snail exploded on the Ningaloo Reef in the 1980s. Surveys of the snails have been undertaken by the Department of Conservation and Land Management in 1989, 1991 and 1993. Although these surveys have shown large variations of population densities of the snails at different sites, there has been little change in total numbers of snails throughout the region. There is no doubt that outbreaks of *Drupella cornus* significantly impact on the coral reef, and it is important that this research work is continued so we can fully understand the impact of the snail's activities.

# Slugs of the sea

You would be unlucky if you have dived or snorkelled at Coral Bay and not seen at least one nudibranch (pronounced 'noo-dee-brank'). Or perhaps you were not looking for these sea slugs, many of which have bizarre shapes and are brightly coloured. Most divers find their striking colours and patterns captivating. Some even take pictures of them as avidly as others collect sea shells. A diversity of species are found in the Ningaloo Marine Park.

Sea slugs are a form of the gastropod molluscs called opisthobranches, which include bubble shells, sea hares, side-gilled sea slugs and others. Nudibranchs, however, have lost all trace of a shell. Their name means 'naked gill' and is an apt description of most species.

In the most diverse group of nudibranchs, the dorids, a circle or semi-circle of brightly-coloured feathery appendages has replaced internal gills. They protrude from the animal's back and circle the anus. When disturbed, some species can retract these gills into an opening known as the branchial pocket. Other species that lack a pocket contract their gills into a clump.

Another group of nudibranchs also has 'naked gills', but these are located on the underside of the body. They are arranged in leaflets that may number up to 100.

Aeolid nudibranchs lack distinct gills and use finger-like protrusions called cerata for respiration, digestion and defence. Cerata often cover the entire upper surface of the animal, making aeolids some of the most flamboyant and colourful nudibranchs.

Above: *Nudibranch eggs. There may be up to one million eggs in this colourful mass.*
*Photo - Vivien Matson-Larkin*
Below: *The feathery appendages on the back on this nudibranch are its gills. Photo - Sue Morrison*

Two prominent appendages, called rhinophores, protrude like antennae from the head of the nudibranch. These organs can detect touch, chemicals and light in the water. Sometimes nudibranchs have two pairs of rhinophores, or a pair of more ordinary-looking tentacles in front of the rhinophores. Others have tentacles at the sides of the mouth, which can be elaborate, and feather-like projections that can be retracted if danger threatens.

Nudibranchs are carnivores and, depending on the family and species, often feed on highly specific prey. This may include eggs of other molluscs, sponges, or cnidarians such as corals, anemones and hydroids. The radula of most nudibranchs is a ribbon of teeth. The structure of this organ varies considerably between species, and helps to distinguish between the various groups of nudibranchs. In general, however, the teeth are arranged in rows and new teeth are continually being added from the rear to replace worn ones at the front.

## Staying alive

You may think that, without a shell, a slow-moving nudibranch is very vulnerable to predators. These animals have, however, evolved many ingenious methods to deter enemies. Some species have camouflaged themselves by assuming the colour of their favourite food. For example, a bright pink nudibranch (*Verconia verconis*) has a remarkably similar appearance to the bright pink sponge on which it feeds. Others display contrasting colours to warn off predators. Of these, some produce a foul-

*A Spanish dancer, one of the larger nudibranchs. Photo - Vivien Matson-Larkin*

*The gills of this nudibranch* (Phyllidiella pustulosa) *consist of up to 100 leaflets along the underside of the body. Photo - Sue Morrison*

tasting acid secretion and are quickly spat out by fish, which soon learn not to sample them again. Others do not produce unpalatable chemicals, but mimic those that do.

Some aeolid nudibranchs feed on corals, hydroids and anemones and are able to store the stinging cells (nematocysts) of these creatures within their own tissue. The nematocysts are transported to the cerata, where they will sting any unfortunate predator that takes a mouthful. The nudibranch then crawls away, leaving the predator in great discomfort, as the nematocysts may continue to sting for a considerable length of time.

## Reproducing

Sea slugs are hermaphrodites, having both male and female sexual organs. They do not, however, self-fertilise, and sperm sacs are exchanged during copulation. Copulation may last for a few seconds or up to several hours, depending on the species. In some, the genital organs are visible as the sea slugs join side to side.

Eggs are laid in a colourful mass that may resemble a ribbon-like strand arranged in a spiral. This 'ribbon' may be narrow, or wide and ruffled. Some have been likened to a fully opened rose. Larger nudibranch species are capable of laying up to one million eggs in the mass. The young of some may hatch as juvenile replicas of their parents, while others hatch as larvae with a shell and operculum that are later cast off. Sea slugs usually have a short life span. Some nudibranchs which eat short-lived prey are themselves short-lived and may only survive for a few weeks, or less. Other species may live for up to a year.

## Solar-powered

One of the most bizarre features of some sea slugs is their ability to utilise microscopic, single-celled algae called zooxanthellae as a food source. Zooxanthellae live embedded in the tissues of many marine organisms, and are responsible for the colour we see in corals, giant clams and many of the hydroids and anemones inhabiting the reef.

Several aeolid nudibranchs ingest the zooxanthellae when feeding on their prey. They store the algae in their own body tissues, especially within the cerata. Due to their shape and position on the slug's back, the cerata have a large surface area directed at the sun – forming the perfect mobile solar collector! Through the process of sun-induced photosynthesis, the zooxanthellae produce energy-rich nutrients as a by-product which the sea slug uses to supplement its diet. As the zooxanthellae die, they are absorbed and replaced by the slug as it continues to graze.

## Finding nudibranchs

At Coral Bay, you can spot nudibranchs in less than a metre of water while snorkelling. The most colourful can be seen from several metres away, but it takes more practise to find the cleverly camouflaged individuals. If you are diving, sit for a while in front of a coral outcrop and wait for movement, or check under rocks or coral. Always replace the rock afterwards. Many nudibranchs are nocturnal, so include a few night dives in your plans. The animals are often more easily seen at night, since the torch beam concentrates on a small area at a time.

Remember that, although these creatures have amazing defence strategies against most of their predators, they are soft-bodied animals that can easily be crushed between fingers. If you do touch a nudibranch, do so gently. Let it crawl on the palm of your hand, marvel at its grace and beauty, then return it to the surface from which it came. It may have been in the middle of digesting another scoop of zooxanthellae or nematocysts to convert to energy or defence – something that our tissues will probably never be able to do.

# Bivalves

Bivalves, including clams, oysters and mussels, usually have two shells (valves). The valves may be a similar size and shape, as in most clams, or uneven, as in some scallops that have one flattened and one rounded valve. These are joined by a flexible ligament and are hinged, usually having interlocking teeth and pits that provide efficient closure of the shell.

## Clams and oysters

Giant clams (*Tridacna maxima* and *Tridacna squamosa*) are among the best known and impressive bivalves on the coral reef. Many are found on the outer reef and in shallow water at Coral Bay and in the lagoons along the length of Ningaloo Reef. All giant clams and many other members of this group contain microscopic algae, known as zooxanthellae, in their mantles. The algae produce food that can also be used by the clam. These microscopic plants contribute to the beautiful colours and patterns of the clam's mantle. Clams also have light and pressure-sensitive spots that look like a row of eyes along the edge of the mantle. This is why clams close quite quickly at any type of disturbance, such as a diver swimming overhead.

Many other bivalves, such as the thorny oyster (*Spondylus varius*), also have very colourful mantles and sensitive spots. They are usually found cemented to the reef or burrowing in the sea floor.

Above: *Like clams, oysters also have colourful mantles. Photo - Ann Storrie*
Below: *Giant clams are very common in the Ningaloo Marine Park and can be seen in shallow water within the lagoons. Photo - Bill Brogan*

*This octopus blends in well with the surrounding reef. Photo - Sue Morrison*

# Cephalopods

There are more than 650 species of cephalopods known from around the world, but relatively few of these inhabit coral reefs. This class of molluscs includes octopuses, squid, cuttlefish and the chambered nautilus. The word 'cephalopod' is derived from the Greek term for 'head-foot', and refers to the animals' suckered tentacles, which appear to be joined to the head.

The nautilus, with its chambered pearly shell, is one of the most primitive cephalopods, and resembles ammonites, creatures which dominated the seas millions of years ago. The nautilus lives at great depths and prefers tropical waters. You may never see a live nautilus, but may be lucky enough to find an empty shell bobbing on the surface of the water in the Ningaloo Marine Park.

## Remarkable reproduction

Cephalopods have separate sexes and reproduce sexually, although they do it a little differently to other animals. Males package their sperm in packets called spermatophores that pass along a groove in a specialised arm with a reduced number of suckers. With this arm, the male places a spermatophore into the female's mantle cavity. The packet explodes and a million or more sperm swim to the female's ovary. When the eggs are laid, they are laden with yolk so that the young can be well formed before they hatch.

## Intelligent invertebrates

Have you ever communicated with an octopus? It has one of the most advanced nervous systems of all invertebrate animals. Next time you meet one underwater, stretch out your arm to shake hands. After a minute, the octopus may reply by stretching out one of its eight arms, gripping your hand and pulling you towards its lair. It is wise to shake hands with a small octopus, though keep clear of those with blue rings!

The nervous system and sensory organs of cephalopods are designed to assess and respond quickly to danger. Their vision is similar to that of people, and they have acute senses of taste and touch. They also have nervous control over blood vessels, enabling them to constrict blood flow to severed arms to decrease bleeding.

By stretching and contracting cells of coloured pigment in their skin, octopuses, squid and cuttlefish can quickly change colour to express aggression, fear or sexual arousal, or to blend in with their surroundings. Many cephalopods can also alter the texture of their skin by raising projections on the skin to give them a larger, more spiky appearance. This is particularly apparent in octopuses and cuttlefish.

Their ability to change colour means cephalopods are masters of disguise. Added to this, octopuses can squeeze their shell-less bodies into tiny holes and crevices in the reef. Unless you are attuned to their habits and are specifically looking for them, most will be overlooked during a dive. One of the smallest is the blue-ringed octopus, which often lives in empty shells, under rocks, in crevices in the reef, or in litter such as bottles and cans. There are at least three species in Western Australia. When undisturbed, blue-ringed octopuses are coloured in shades of brown and black. Only when they become excited do their vivid blue bands, rings or spots show out against the dark patches of skin. They can inject tetrodotoxin – one of the deadliest poisons known –

Above: *A cuttlefish. Photo - Ann Storrie*
Below: *Squids are often seen in large schools swimming through the lagoons of the Ningaloo Marine Park.*
*Photo - Vivien Matson-Larkin*

which causes paralysis and often death in humans. Most people are bitten while handling a shell or bottle housing a blue-ringed octopus. If you see one, treat it with respect and do not touch it.

Cuttlefish and their close relatives, dumpling squid, are often seen in the Ningaloo Marine Park. They are well adapted to swimming close to the bottom in search of prey. Cuttlefish have a large, flat, internal shell which is the familiar cuttlebone found washed up on beaches. This is used for regulating buoyancy. The density of the cuttlebone can be changed by pumping liquid in and out of tiny chambers within it, thereby altering the volume of the gas-filled space. Dumpling squid lack shells.

Squid, on the other hand, are adapted for life in mid-water. Large schools of squid are often seen swimming through the marine park. They are a little like a slim-line, high-speed cuttlefish that hunts fast-moving schools of fish. Their cuttlebone has been replaced with a thin, lightweight, transparent, horny structure that supports the tissues.

# Shrimps, crabs and lobsters

*Crustaceans range from large lobsters and crabs to microscopic organisms that drift about as part of the plankton. Some live as parasites in or on fish and invertebrates.*

Crustaceans generally have a hard, jointed external skeleton, called an exoskeleton, and three distinct body segments - a head, thorax and abdomen. Their legs are also jointed and can move in nearly every direction. At some stage of their lives, crustaceans have two pairs of antennae, unlike other arthropods which only have one pair. Many also have specialised appendages, such as claws and maxillipeds, to handle and shred food.

There are two main groups. Most large crustaceans, such as crabs and lobsters, belong to the Order Decapoda, which means ten legs. Barnacles, amphipods, isopods such as sea lice, and several other small, shrimp-like creatures are known as non-decapods.

Shrimps, crabs and lobsters are the most well known decapod crustaceans. Up to three pairs of their legs are modified as maxillipeds that are often termed 'mouth parts', and which shred food and place it into the mouth. At least one other pair of legs ends in a claw that is used for catching and picking up food.

To grow, these crustaceans must shed their exoskeleton and replace it with a larger one. This process of moulting (ecdysis) involves producing a new, soft skeleton inside the old one. When ready, the animal discards its old shell, then quickly increases in size by taking up water before the new exoskeleton hardens. This allows room for normal growth of the animal over the next few months until it needs to moult again.

## Prawns and shrimps

The term prawn is sometimes applied to crustaceans that possess a longer, serrated rostrum or beak that projects from the shell. In Australia, large shrimps are generally known as prawns. You will find hundreds of them on the reef if you look closely. Many tropical species of cleaner shrimps, such as the banded coral shrimp (*Stenopus hispidus*), are found at Ningaloo. They may live in permanent cleaning stations on the reef, where fish

Left: *Banded coral shrimp.*
Right: *Shrimp in anemone.*
*Photos - Vivien Matson-Larkin*

visit to be cleaned. Others are found living in a crevice with a moray eel. The eel benefits from being cleaned by the shrimp, and the shrimp picks up food scraps left by the eel.

Another symbiotic relationship involves small gobies and alpheid shrimps. The shrimp digs and maintains a burrow in which they both reside, and the goby watches for predators. Apparently, alpheid shrimps have poor eyesight. Some species of shrimps live within the stinging tentacles of anemones. They receive protection from predators, while the shrimp cleans the anemone. These shrimps are often brightly coloured, but are usually very small.

# Crabs

Most people are familiar with the larger species of crabs, especially the blue manna crab (*Portunus pelagicus*). It is found in bays and estuaries with sandy bottoms all around Australia. On reefs such as Ningaloo there are also thousands of small, sometimes insignificant crabs that lie camouflaged in corals, sponges, anemones and seagrasses. Other species of crabs live in the intertidal zones, and can be seen on rocks above the water line, or on beaches where they forage for food not far from their burrows. Due to their confusing classifications, only a few of the more interesting crabs are described here under their common names.

## Hermit crabs

Hermit crabs inhabit discarded mollusc shells. Unlike most other crustaceans, they do not have a hard exoskeleton on their abdomen. The animal protects itself by sliding its long, soft abdomen into an empty mollusc shell, and carrying the shell on its back

*Tropical reef crab in the Family Xanthidae. Photo - Ann Storrie*

*Hermit crabs live in discarded mollusc shells. Photo - Bill Brogan*

wherever it goes. As the crab grows, it simply finds a larger shell and swaps houses. Many species have beautifully marked and coloured legs and eyes, though patience is required to photograph them. They can usually retract completely into their portable home.

## Reef crabs

Reef crabs from the Family Xanthidae come in all sizes. Many have bright colours and patterns symmetrically distributed on their carapace, but are often toxic if consumed by people. Others, like the hairy coral crabs, are inconspicuous among the corals, as they carry a camouflaging coat of algae.

## Decorator crabs

Decorator crabs may coat themselves completely in debris or other animals, and are almost completely invisible in their chosen habitat. Their carapace is usually covered with spines and has hooked hairs. The crab chooses whatever affords the best camouflage and attaches it to these hairs. If it lives in an area of bright blue sponges, for instance, the crab will 'plant' pieces of the sponge on its legs and back. The sponge then continues to grow on the crab, and probably benefits from its newfound, mobile existence. Other decorator crabs may wear a garden of soft coral, bryozoans, algae and even anemones. The crabs will sometimes also eat the camouflage, so you could say they carry a larder on their backs.

## Spider crabs

Many spider crabs belong to the same family as decorator crabs and will often use materials from their habitat to coat their bodies. Many are very small and difficult to find, even if they have not pinched additional material for camouflage. Some simply resemble the colour of the corals on which they live.

As their name suggests, they look more like spiders than crabs. They usually have long, slender legs, and perch like a jumping spider on top of corals. One species, however, has an elongated body with short legs, and lives on gorgonian corals. Many species are yet to be identified, and there are probably many more still waiting to be discovered.

### Sponge crabs

Sponge crabs have a small pair of back legs with hook-like claws to hold a cup-shaped sponge or ascidian on their back. The crab is almost enveloped by the sponge and usually overlooked by divers. Some are quite large, growing to about 20 centimetres wide. They are nearly always sluggish and depend almost entirely on their camouflage for defence.

### Anemone crabs

Like some species of shrimps, a number of crab species live in and under anemones. An attractive group known as the porcelain crabs are found on many anemones. Next time you come across an anemone in Coral Bay, or on the outer reef, gently touch one side. The anemone will fold up and you may see several tiny crabs scurrying for cover.

## Lobsters

Western Australia's best known lobster is the western rock lobster *(Panulirus cygnus)*, commonly known as the crayfish (although the term is more correctly applied to freshwater species). Its range extends from Augusta to Onslow. During the crayfishing season, crays may be taken by people who hold recreational fishing permits, but only in areas outside the park's sanctuary zones.

Two other colourful species of rock lobsters are found at Ningaloo Reef and in waters further north. The painted rock lobster *(Panulirus versicolor)* is usually bluish-green, with a white reticulated pattern on its carapace, and grows up to 40 centimetres long. The ornate rock lobster *(Panulirus ornatus)* can grow slightly larger, and often has distinctive dark and light blotches on its legs. A species of double-spined rock lobster *(Panulirus penicillatus)*, may also be found at Ningaloo, but is not common.

Another lobster that does not resemble our 'crayfish' is the slipper or flat lobster *(Scyllarides squammosus)*. It is slow-moving and has a flattened carapace with weakly-spined edges. Slipper lobsters can reach about 40 centimetres long.

## Barnacles, lice and planktonic crustaceans

Non-decapod crustaceans do not have ten legs. The barnacles are probably the best known. Although they do not look like crustaceans, barnacles have free-swimming larvae that have crustacean characteristics. As an adult, the barnacle's typical jointed appendages have become modified as feeding cirri, and their external skeleton has become a series of plates. They attach themselves to marine invertebrates (such as sponges, gorgonians and hard corals), rocks, and floating timbers and fixtures such as the Exmouth Jetty.

Another non-decapod sometimes seen on the reef is the mantis shrimp. It grows up to 30 centimetres long, is very colourful, and has powerful claws used to catch and

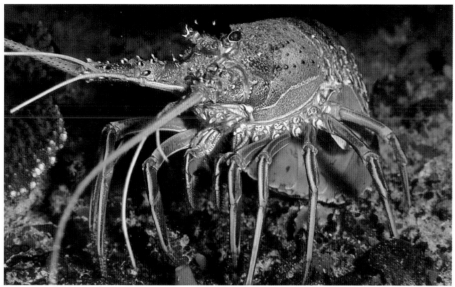

*Western rock lobster. Photo - Ann Storrie*

smash the shells of other crustaceans. It will also prey on fish, molluscs and worms. If you find a mantis shrimp, do not poke your finger at it, or in its hole. You may end up with a broken finger, or your camera lens may be shattered if you zoom in too close!

Isopods, such as marine lice, grow to about four centimetres long and are usually attached to the sides of fish, especially damselfish. Others live buried inside sponges. By far the most numerous non-decapods are small, microscopic planktonic animals such as copepods, euphausids and the larvae of other crustaceans (for example, crabs). These planktonic crustaceans (together with the larvae of fish and various marine invertebrates) occur in large numbers in the open ocean, in crevices within the reef and among rubble and sand. They are collectively known as zooplankton and feed on minute plants, known as phytoplankton. The zooplankton play a very important role in the overall ecology of coral reefs, forming the main food source for many other invertebrates and juvenile fish.

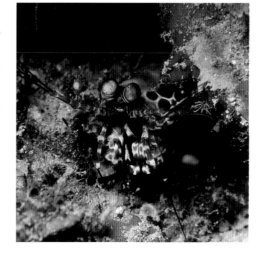

*Mantis shrimps have powerful claws that can smash the shells of molluscs and other invertebrates.*
*Photo - Ann Storrie*

# Bryozoans:
# cryptic criters

*There are more than 4000 species of bryozoans in our oceans, very few of which are easily recognised by divers. This is hardly surprising, since bryozoans closely resemble many other marine plants and invertebrates, such as algae, corals, hydroids and sponges.*

A colony of bryozoans is made up of tiny animals called zooids, in the Phylum Bryozoa. The zooids are usually too small to be seen clearly without a microscope. However, each zooid is quite complex, and has a digestive system, nervous system and a muscular system. They usually live attached to rocks or other suitable surfaces, including the hulls of boats, and bryozoans are often the first to colonise a bare surface.

A common bryozoan that is easily recognised at Ningaloo Reef is the 'lace coral' bryozoan. It usually grows in a circular form, is hard and brittle, and looks like lace. It comes in a variety of colours, but is often white or pale orange. Occasionally, a colony may boast two or three attractive colours within the structure. Lace coral bryozoans have a high calcium component in their structure that gives them their rigidity. Other bryozoans, however, have the flexibility and consistency of plants. It is sometimes quite difficult to differentiate between algae and bryozoans. Algae must have light to photosynthesise, so if the specimen is beneath a rock or ledge, or in a dark cave, it is probably a bryozoan. Like encrusting sponges, some bryozoans also form a thin layer of cells over rocks and debris. Some even grow on other animals, including shells.

Bryozoans play a significant role in the ecology of the marine environment. They feed on plankton, and are food for many other invertebrates. Some nudibranchs and sea spiders feed only on bryozoans. Bryozoans also compete with other animals, such as sponges and ascidians, for positions on the reef.

Bryozoans can reproduce by budding or by sexual reproduction. Some species are self-fertilising. They shed sperm and eggs into a hollow body cavity, where fertilisation occurs. The eggs develop into larvae, which are expelled as free-swimming organisms that finally attach to an underwater surface to start a new colony of bryozoans.

Left: *This bryozoan is soft and flexible.*
*Photo - Sue Morrison*
Right: *A 'lace coral' bryozoan.*
*Photo - Ann Storrie*

# Sea stars, urchins and their relatives

*Sea stars, brittle stars, feather stars, sea urchins and sea cucumbers are all echinoderms, which means spiny-skinned animals. The name is derived from the Greek word echinos, a hedgehog.*

Although some echinoderms outwardly resemble a hedgehog, others are quite different. All, however, have a calcareous skeleton of plates or tiny ossicles. Sea urchins and some sea stars have spiny protrusions, while sea cucumbers have a smooth, almost fleshy skin. Microscopic examination is necessary to view the numerous plates, or ossicles, in the body wall of the fleshy echinoderms.

Echinoderms are radially symmetrical. This means that if they are divided through the mouth and down the body length, the two halves will be identical (in bilaterally symmetrical bodies, such as ours, the right and left halves will be similar but not identical). All echinoderms also have extendable, hollow tube feet with suction-like tips. Water is ducted to the tube feet by way of a system of canals, like a circulatory system. The control is so delicately balanced, that the tube feet can be retracted or extended, or waved about in any direction in a very flexible manner.

## Sea stars

Of the five classes of echinoderms, sea stars (starfish) are probably the best known. Most have five arms, although some species have seven or more. They feed on a variety of invertebrates such as sponges, ascidians and organic debris. Some are able to open bivalves, such as oysters, by pulling gently but steadily on the shells with their tube feet. Eventually the mollusc's muscle tires and the shells open. The sea star is then able to evert its stomach to surround the flesh of the mollusc and digest it.

Sea stars have amazing powers of regeneration. Some, if cut in two, will survive to become two sea stars. Some species actually reproduce this way. A few can regrow from an arm if it is detached, forming a comet-shaped individual.

Sea stars also reproduce sexually. Eggs and sperm are produced in gonads within the arms. When spawning, the gonads of some species increase in size to almost the entire length of the arms. The spawn is

Left: *Photo - Ann Storrie*
Right: *Blue sea star (*Linckia laevigata*).*
*Photo - Peter and Margy Nicholas*

then liberated into the sea, close to another spawning sea star. Sexes are usually separate, but hermaphrodite individuals are sometimes found.

Most sea stars can be safely handled. An exception is the crown-of-thorns, a large sea star up to 60 centimetres across. It is usually bluish grey, though some are bright purple or red. This animal has stout, hinged spines, two to three centimetres long, each with a three-sided blade at the tip. These are covered with a thin skin that produces venom and mucus. Avoid handling these animals, even with gloves, as a puncture wound from a spine is intensely painful and can lead to infection. The crown-of-thorns has destroyed large areas of coral on the Great Barrier Reef and in the Indo-Pacific. It is quite rare in Ningaloo Marine Park, and, although you may find some in Coral Bay and on the outer reef, they have done little harm to corals in Western Australia, except off Dampier.

## Brittle stars

Brittle stars are the most numerous and successful echinoderms, but these nocturnal secretive animals are not as easily seen as sea stars. Like sea stars, they have a central disc with a mouth on the underside. Their arms are generally longer, and more flexible, than sea stars and their tube feet lack adhesive suckers. Instead, they trap plankton and organic debris in mucus that covers their tube feet. Many brittle stars hide under rocks and coral slabs by day. At night, you may

come across one or two arms that resemble worms meandering across the coral or sand. If you trace this back to a rock and peek underneath, you may find a brittle star that has sent out an arm in search of food.

Two specialised types of brittle star - basket stars and serpent stars - are often in full view, but may not be recognised as echinoderms by divers. Basket stars are nocturnal animals with huge, spreading arms that form a net to catch plankton. The net is made up of tiny, complex branched arms, and may measure up to 60 centimetres across. Basket stars are usually found in areas subject to strong currents. During the day, their arms are coiled into a tight knot that looks more like a rope stuck to the rock than a basket star. Serpent stars are usually found wrapped around the 'stem' of a black coral. They may

*Crinoids, or feather stars, are relatives of sea stars.*
*Photo - Ann Storrie*

look like one long strand of rope, but usually consist of five arms that can be unravelled and stretched out like 'normal' brittle star arms.

## Feather stars

Feather stars (crinoids), so-named because of their feather-like arms, come in all colours of the rainbow. Some have bright yellow or red arms, others are green, black or orange, and some seem to almost fluoresce with brilliant purple or dark blue. They are predominantly nocturnal, but their bright arms are often seen curled between crevices in the reef during the day. At night, they may perch on top of coral, to capture passing plankton for food.

Feather stars differ from sea stars and brittle stars in several ways. Their stomach is on top of the body, rather than beneath, and the tube feet have been modified into types of tentacles on the arms. These help to sweep food into grooves that run down each arm towards the mouth. Like sea stars, their anus is also on the dorsal surface, but is elevated in a cone. Feather stars can move about

*Sea urchins are like 'hedgehogs' of the ocean. Photo - Vivien Matson-Larkin*

and attach themselves to the rock by means of leg-like projections called cirri. Some can even 'swim' by waving their arms up and down.

The tentacles on the arms give the animal a feathery appearance. They are also coated with mucus that helps it to catch food. Tiny hooks on the arms stick to wetsuits and gloves, and many divers find crinoids stuck to them after a dive. If this occurs, gently pull the crinoid and its arms off and return them to the water.

## Sea urchins

Many divers have spent considerable time pulling sea urchin spines from their skin. A diadema urchin is a real 'hedgehog' of the ocean, with long, fine black spines that penetrate all thicknesses of wetsuits and gloves. Be especially careful at night, when they can form a carpet as they move across the sand in search of food. Despite their awesome defence, these sea urchins are still vulnerable to predatory fish such as triggerfish and pufferfish.

The flower urchin (*Toxopneustes pileolus*) can also cause severe pain, and even unconsciousness. Numerous short spines are hidden in a rosette of flower-like pedicellariae that are pincer-like organs. It is these, rather than the spines, that cause damage. Each pedicellariae is a rounded triangular shape with three fangs that make up a jaw. When sensory hairs inside the jaws are stimulated, the jaws close and inject venom through the fangs. The venom interferes with nerve-muscle coordination and paralyses the muscle.

Not all sea urchins are dangerous. Pencil urchins have large, rounded spines that resemble slate-pencils. If you pick one up, examine the base of the spines. They provide one of the best examples of ball-and-socket joints in the animal kingdom.

# Heart urchins and sand dollars

Heart urchins and sand dollars are specialised sea urchins. Heart urchins are shaped a little like an Australian football and have short spines covering the body. There are several species, all of which live under the sand and are often found in the shallows of Coral Bay.

Sand dollars, urchins with very flattened bodies and a sea star insignia on the upper side, lie just under the sandy surface of the sea floor and an experienced eye can often detect them by their outline. They have numerous tube feet and very tiny spines. One species is common on sand flats in the Bay of Rest, Exmouth Gulf.

# Sea cucumbers

Sea cucumbers are so unlike typical echinoderms that it is hard to believe they are closely related. Some are sausage-shaped, leathery-skinned creatures, some are

small, colourful creatures, while others are long and thin, and are often mistaken for worms as they move around rocks and across the sand. Sea cucumbers also have several names including holothurians, beche-de-mer and trepang. All sea cucumbers, however, have the calcareous ossicles that characterise echinoderms.

The large sea cucumbers with leathery skins usually browse on the sea floor, moving slowly on their tube feet. They ingest great quantities of sand, from which they extract edible, organic matter. The waste is left in a trail behind the animal, as it slowly travels over the sea bed. If disturbed, some eject sticky tubules as a means of defence. These can irritate the skin and cause severe pain if accidentally rubbed into the eyes. This does not deter Indonesian fishermen, who collect them to dry and sell to the

*The tentacles of small colourful sea cucumbers are extended to catch plankton.*
*Photo - Peter and Margy Nicholas*

*This sand dollar skeleton clearly shows the typical sea star insignia. Photo - Ann Storrie*

Chinese for food. The fishermen once used to collect them as far south as Coral Bay. The small, attractive sea cucumbers that attach themselves to rocks feed by means of colourful tentacles. After plankton is trapped in the tentacles, the sea cucumbers fold these appendages into their mouths to remove the food. The long, thin sea cucumbers move over the sea floor, not by tube feet, but by anchor-shaped ossicles in the skin, and feed by sweeping their tentacles across the sand. Other tiny sea cucumbers live on barrel sponges, and apparently feed on substances secreted by the sponge.

*Black sea cucumbers use their tube feet to move across the bottom, picking up food particles. Photo - Bill Brogan*

# Sea squirts

*Many a diver's log book contains a treasure trove of mistaken identities. One group of animals, the sea squirts or ascidians, are particularly misunderstood and misnamed. They have been recorded as sponges, algae, corals, flowers and even eggs that have hatched.*

Ascidians are commonly called sea squirts because of the jet of water that is often expelled from the body openings when you touch them. Surprisingly, they belong to the Phylum Chordata, the same phylum that includes humans. Not that they resemble mammals. However, during their larval stage, sea squirts have a tail that is strengthened with a rod of cartilage that is similar to the backbone in a tadpole. They also have a nerve cord that is a feature of all vertebrates. These free-swimming larvae, or tadpoles, also have a light-sensing spot, and gill slits similar to fish and juvenile amphibians. After the larva has completed its swimming stage, which is usually less than six hours, it attaches its 'face' to a rock surface and undergoes metamorphosis. The tail is absorbed, the body openings enlarge to form siphons, and the pharynx (the area just behind the mouth) enlarges and a leathery body covering called the tunic is secreted. The word 'ascidian' originated from the Greek term 'askos', which can be translated to 'leather wine bag'.

## Shapes and form

The young sea squirt will either live as a solitary individual or in close association with others, depending on the species. Solitary forms live independently of other ascidians. Some of these are known as sea tulips. The body of a sea tulip can grow up to 20 centimetres long and is held at the end of a long stalk attached to the reef.

Colonial sea squirts consist of individual animals called zooids. They are usually connected by branches called stolons that allow fluids to flow between them. An example is the blue-throated ascidian. It is common under ledges on the outer reef of Ningaloo Marine Park, and can be seen on the piles of Exmouth Jetty.

Alternatively, a closer association known as a compound ascidian is formed.

Left: *Colonial ascidians.*
Photo - *Bill Brogan*
Right: *A compound ascidian.*
Photo - *Ann Storrie*

This consists of numerous individual animals that share a common tunic and common system of waste-water flow. Some of these form colourful, intricate patterns on the reef. Others are almost indistinguishable from encrusting sponges. Generally, however, their siphons are less randomly placed than sponges, and they respond to pressure and light by closing and retracting their siphons.

# Filter feeders

Like sponges, sea squirts are filter feeders. However, their mechanism for extracting and absorbing food particles is far more complex. They have two siphons, one to take in water and another to expel water and wastes. These are obvious in solitary sea squirts with large siphons. The inhalant siphon of compound sea squirts is also obvious, but their exhalant siphon opens into large internal spaces or canals within the colony.

To draw water into their inhalant siphons, sea squirts have tiny hairs called cilia within their large body cavity, the pharynx. The cilia are continually beating, moving water into the pharynx, where tiny food particles such as plankton and bacteria are extracted. The food particles are directed into streams of mucus that pass up each side of the pharynx. Filtered water is then passed into another chamber called the atrium, from where it is expelled via the exhalant siphon. The food in the mucus is passed into a stomach, where it is digested and the nutrients transported via a rudimentary circulatory system to the rest of the body. Wastes are passed from the stomach to the atrium, where they too are excreted via the exhalant siphon. The exhalant siphon is always positioned so that the waste does not contaminate the water coming into the inhalant siphon.

*Solitary sea squirts are a little like small wine bags stuck on the reef. Photo - Vivien Matson-Larkin*

*Attractive blue and yellow colonial ascidians. Photo - Sue Morrison*

# The sex life of a sea squirt

The method of reproduction depends on the species. Solitary sea squirts release ova or sperm into the water through their exhalant siphons. Fertilisation then occurs at random, and the embryo develops into free-swimming larva while drifting in the current. Some solitary sea squirts are hermaphrodites, but they avoid self-fertilisation by producing sperm and ova at different times. Other solitary sea squirts are of either male or female gender.

Colonial and compound sea squirts can also reproduce sexually, but by internal fertilisation. Sperm enters a zooid containing eggs, and the young are incubated in the zooid until they have become tailed larvae. They are then released to swim around for about 10 minutes before attaching themselves to underwater surfaces and undergoing metamorphosis. Colonial groups also reproduce asexually. The zooids may divide, or bud off more zooids, thus increasing the size of the colony.

# Beauty and texture

Sea squirts are beautiful marine creatures that deserve recognition. Next time you see a large, solitary sea squirt, look through one of its siphons. You may be able to see the gill slits that filter the water. In some transparent species you can see the circulatory system, or network of capillaries between the gill slits. These vessels collect oxygen as it diffuses from the passing water. If you are not sure whether you are looking at a sea squirt or sponge, touch it gently on a siphon. If it is a sea squirt, the siphon should retract and close rapidly, then slowly open when danger has passed. Even the flat, sheet-like forms of compound sea squirts which encrust the reef, will react to touch. You may even receive a jet of water from the exhalant siphons as the specimen reacts to your attentions.

# Fishy affairs

*Fish occur in many shapes, sizes and colours, from colourful tropical butterflyfish and appealing clownfish to fast-moving, powerful mackerel and large awe-inspiring sharks. They have adapted to a multitude of habitats such as warm and clear coral reef shallows, cold Antarctic waters, silty estuaries, muddy mangroves, fresh water, open ocean and deep sea where no light penetrates.*

More than 20,000 species of fish have been described so far and around half of these live in shallow seas. Approximately 80 per cent of these shallow water fish live in warm temperate or tropical waters.

Fish are divided into two major groups, distinguished by the structure of their skeleton: the sharks and rays (or cartilaginous fish) and the bony fish. Sharks and rays have a skeleton composed of cartilage and bony fish have a bony skeleton.

## Biology of sharks and rays

Sharks and rays are less advanced in evolutionary terms than the bony fish. Of the 20,000 species of fish described, only about 950 species are sharks and rays. Most sharks and rays are marine, but a few live in estuaries or fresh water.

True sharks have a streamlined body, well suited to these fast swimming, predatory fish. Rays are adapted for life on the bottom and most have a flattened body.

Sharks and rays have primitive, small, pointed scales. New scales develop between the old ones as sharks grow, so scales cannot be used to age sharks and rays. Some cartilaginous fish, such as rays, have lost their scales and instead have a protective coat of mucus over the skin. The teeth have evolved from the pointed scales and are continuously replaced throughout life (like a conveyor belt, growing from just inside the jaw). The best known shark teeth are the large, sharp, pointed cutting teeth of powerful predatory sharks, such as white pointers and tiger sharks. These teeth have evolved to eat large prey items such as marine mammals and turtles. In contrast, rays have plates of flattened teeth that can crush invertebrates such as molluscs and

Left: *A pink anemonefish.*
Photo - *Peter and Margy Nicholas*
Right: *Grey reef shark.*
Photo - *Vivien Matson-Larkin*

crabs. Even more unusual are those of plankton feeders such as whale sharks, basking sharks and manta rays. These fish have only very small teeth, but have modified denticles on each gill arch used to filter plankton from the water.

Sharks and rays have no cover (operculum) over the gills, and the five to seven gill slits are visible on each side of the head. The mouth and nostrils are usually on the underside of the head.

Males can be identified by a pair of external claspers next to the anus. Fertilisation is internal in all sharks and rays. The majority of sharks give birth to live young, but others lay eggs. For example, some rays produce a leathery, brown, rectangular egg case, sometimes known as a 'mermaid's purse'.

# Biology of bony fish

Bony fish constitute the largest fish group and are highly successful and diverse. They inhabit a wide range of aquatic habitats from marine and estuarine to fresh water, including fast-flowing and still waters. Consequently, they have evolved a tremendous variety of body shapes, adapted to their varied lifestyles, including a streamlined 'standard' body form like that of a herring, laterally compressed (such as that of a butterflyfish), dorso-ventrally flattened (like a flounder), elongated (such as an eel) and round (like a pufferfish). They have an equivalent range of colour patterns, from brightly-coloured angelfish to the perfectly camouflaged stonefish.

Bony fish have a similar body plan to sharks and rays. Their fins, however, have more movement than those of sharks and rays, which enable them to perform fine and accurate manoeuvres.

*A northern wobbegong (*Orectolobus wardi*). Photo - Ann Storrie*

*Cardinalfish. Photo - Ann Storrie*

The bony skeleton is strong, but generally light. The scales also contain bone, are thin and overlap. The scales grow with the fish, which results in annual rings (as in a tree trunk) that can be used for ageing. Some species have lost their scales, such as catfish, eels and anglerfish, while others have modified scales, such as the spines of porcupinefish or the bony plates of seahorses and pipefish.

In bony fish an operculum covers the gills, and so the gill slits cannot be seen externally. A gas bladder is present in many species, but has been lost in others.

In most bony fish fertilisation is external. The female often lays vast numbers of eggs and the male immediately releases sperm over them. In some species the eggs are buoyant and they are thus dispersed over long distances by means of ocean currents, enabling colonisation over wide areas. Other species, such as the clownfish, attach the eggs to underwater surfaces or place them in a nest where the adults guard the young, such as the triggerfish. Some species, such as the cardinalfish, even brood the young in their mouths and in seahorses an extreme situation has evolved in which the male broods the young in a pouch or on the skin of his abdomen.

In some families, such as the wrasses, individuals can change sex. The male baldchin groper, for example, has a 'harem' of several females, but if he dies the dominant female will turn into a male and take his place.

# Ningaloo Marine Park fish

The coral reefs of Ningaloo are home to more than 500 species of fish, and there are likely to be even more undescribed species. The goby family has the greatest number of species on coral reefs. However, gobies are not often seen because they are very small. More evident are the colourful damselfish, butterflyfish and wrasses. Larger fish, such as groper, mackerel, trevally and large sharks, tend to be fewer, both in number of individuals and species. This is understandable when you think of the greater quantity of food the bigger individuals need to survive and therefore the larger area of reef needed to support them. Some common families in the Ningaloo Marine Park are described in further detail below.

# Small coral reef fish

## Damselfish

When you first snorkel in the lagoon areas of the Ningaloo Marine Park, you are likely to be impressed by the huge number of damselfish. These are the small, attractive fish which usually congregate around branching corals. When danger approaches, they dart into the coral for safety. Some common species you will see at Coral Bay and Ningaloo are the lemon damsel (*Pomacentrus moluccensis*), black axil chromis (*Chromis atripectoralis*), neon damsel (*Pomacentrus coelestis*), jewel damsel (*Plectroglyphidodon lacrymatus*), scissortail sergeant (*Abudefduf sexfasciatus*) and various species of *Dascyllus* and demoiselles (*Neopomacentrus* spp.). This family of fish is one of the most abundant on coral reefs. Many are highly territorial, particularly the dark brown western gregory (*Stegastes obreptus*). It lays eggs on the bottom which are guarded by the male.

## Clownfish

The most familiar species in the damselfish family are the clownfish or anemonefish. These appealing fish live in close association (symbiosis) with anemones. The anemones often nestle in a hollow in the coral or reef. The four species you are likely to see are Clark's anemonefish (*Amphiprion clarkii*), the pink anemonefish (*Amphiprion perideraion*), the orange anemonefish (*Amphiprion sandaracinos*) and the red anemonefish (*Amphiprion rubrocinctus*), which only occurs in the north-west of Australia. Clownfish continuously move around, either hiding in the anemone or bravely swimming out towards you or other fish, in defence of their territories. Clownfish live in family groups, often one family per anemone. The largest dominant individual is usually a female and the next biggest is the male. Several

*Longfin bannerfish (*Heniochus acuminatus*).
Photo - Peter and Margy Nicholas*

*Clark's anemonefish* (Amphiprion clarkii) *attending its orange eggs. Photo - Ann Storrie*

smaller non-breeding individuals complete the family. An incredible transformation occurs if the female dies; the male changes sex and takes over her role and the largest non-breeding fish develops into a male! This strategy ensures that there is always a pair of adults ready to breed and no time is lost looking for a new mate.

The close association between clownfish and anemones is thought to benefit both partners. The fish gains protection from predators by hiding among the stinging tentacles. A coat of mucus on the fish's skin is thought to provide immunity from the deadly stings of the anemone. In turn, the clownfish protects the anemone from some predators, such as butterflyfish, which eat anemones. Some anemones can survive successfully without clownfish, but anemones with clownfish are usually healthier than unoccupied ones.

## Butterflyfish

Butterflyfish (Chaetodontidae) can be seen on almost every dive. They are not as numerous as the damselfish, but are easily seen because of their attractive colouration. Many species are found in pairs and may even stay together for life, such as the teardrop butterflyfish (*Chaetodon unimaculatus*), redfin butterflyfish (*Chaetodon trifasciatus*), chevroned butterflyfish (*Chaetodon trifascialis*), ornate butterflyfish (*Chaetodon ornatissimus*) and the racoon butterflyfish (*Chaetodon lunula*). Some species are solitary and others are found in schools, such as the longfin bannerfish (*Heniochus acuminatus*). Many butterflyfish feed on coral polyps, whereas others eat small invertebrates and algae. Some have specialised mouthparts, such as the long-nosed butterflyfish (*Forcipiger flavissimus*), whose elongated mouth enables it to feed on small hydroids, crabs, sea urchin tube feet and the tentacles of tube worms! An interesting feature of many butterflyfish, particularly the juveniles, is a dark spot at the rear of the dorsal fin. This spot acts as a false eye, since an attack from a predator in this region will do less damage than an attack at the head end. The real eye is often disguised by a dark stripe.

## Cardinalfish

Cardinalfish (Apogonidae) are small and not initially obvious, but surprisingly common. They are generally nocturnal and can often be found under ledges or crevices during the day. One species, the infamous gobbleguts (*Apogon rueppellii*), is unusual in that it ranges from the cool waters of the south coast to as far north as the warm waters of New Guinea. It is a pale colour, with a distinctive row of fine black dots along each side. This family is unusual among marine fish in being mouth-brooders. The male incubates the eggs in his mouth for several days until they hatch. You can distinguish these males by their distended throats and you can often see the eggs inside. The ring-tailed cardinalfish (*Apogon aureus*) and the coral cardinalfish (*Apogon properupta*) are commonly seen at Ningaloo.

## Blennies

Although not seen in large numbers, the blennies (Blenniidae) are a large family with some interesting members. These small fish have long, narrow bodies, and a pair of tentacles on the head often crowns an appealing face. Many eat algae and have large, bulbous stomachs, such as the black blenny (*Cirripectes hutchinsi*) and coral blenny (*Ecsenius yaeyamensis*). An intriguing group are the sabretooth blennies. They are carnivorous and have two gigantic canine teeth in the lower jaw. One such species, the false cleaner wrasse (*Aspidontus taeniatus*), mimics the cleaner wrasse, but instead of cleaning parasites off other fish, it bites off pieces of flesh and scales with its huge fangs! Another sabretooth blenny commonly seen is the black-banded blenny (*Meiacanthus grammistes*). It has a venom gland in the canines, which are used only for defence.

## Gobies

The goby family has the largest number of species, but they are generally small in physical size. If you rest quietly on the bottom, you will begin to notice small fish darting around the base of the coral. Many of these are gobies, such as the banded goby (*Amblygobius phalaena*), decorated goby (*Istigobius decoratus*) and ornate goby (*Istigobius ornatus*). Other species hide among the coral branches, including the coral goby (*Gobiodon citrinus*) and tiny whip gobies (*Bryaninops* sp.), which cling to long, slender sea whip corals. Another curious relationship (symbiosis) can be seen between several species of gobies and shrimps, such as Wheeler's shrimp goby (*Amblyeleotris wheeleri*) and alpheid shrimps. A goby pair shares a burrow in the sand with two shrimps. The shrimps dig out and maintain the burrow, but have poor eyesight, and the fish keeps a watch for predators. The shrimps keep in contact with the gobies using their feelers, and can quickly detect danger from the behaviour of the fish.

# Medium-sized coral reef fish

## Angelfish

Angelfish (Pomacanthidae) can easily be confused with butterflyfish. However, unlike butterflyfish, angelfish have an obvious spine at the base of the gill cover (operculum).

Clockwise from top left: *Neon threefin* (Helcogramma striata), *Photo - Peter and Margy Nicholas; blue-green chromis* (Chromis viridis), *Photo - Gerhardt Saueracker; scribbled angelfish* (Chaetodontoplus duboulayi), *Photo - Ann Storrie; striped catfish* (Plotosus lineatus) , *Photo - Sue Morrison; painted sweetlips* (Diagramma labiosum), *Photo - Paul Jelley; and lemon damsel* (Pomacentrus vaiuli), *Photo - Bill Brogan.*

Like butterflyfish, angelfish stand out because of their exquisite colours and patterns, although they do not occur in large numbers. These beautiful fish are frequently timid, and are clever at turning so that only a narrow profile of their rear end is visible. With patience, however, you can be rewarded by the sight of a more inquisitive individual, particularly the blue angelfish (*Pomacanthus semicircularis*) and the keyhole angelfish (*Centropyge tibicen*). More elusive are the emperor angelfish (*Pomacanthus imperator*), the six-banded angelfish (*Pomacanthus sexstriatus*) and Eibl's angelfish (*Centropyge eibli*). It's hard to believe that the juveniles belong to the same family, because their colour patterns are completely different from that of the adults. The juveniles are dark blue, with abstract swirls of white and pale blue lines. These patterns break up the body shape and camouflage the young fish from predators.

## Wrasses

The wrasse family (Labridae) is second only to the gobies in the number of species in Western Australia. The wrasses, however, are much more evident than gobies on the reef, as most are larger and more brightly coloured. Identifying wrasses can be difficult because juveniles, males and females often differ markedly in colour. Many males and females were thought to be different species in the early days of taxonomy. To complicate the matter, sex reversal occurs in many species of wrasse. If a dominant male dies, one of the females will change into a male and take over his role. Wrasses can be distinguished by their curious habit of swimming with just their pectoral fins. The tail is only used for occasional, short bursts of speed. Members of only one other family, the parrotfish, swim in this manner, but they can be distinguished by their teeth, which look like a parrot's beak.

All wrasses are carnivorous, but different species feed on a range of prey, from tiny plankton, coral polyps and invertebrates in the sand to larger molluscs, urchins, crabs and small fish. Some species have teeth in their throat to help crush larger prey items. One wrasse which you will see on nearly every dive has a very specialised method of feeding. This is the cleaner wrasse (*Labroides dimidiatus*), which feeds on parasites attached to the skin and gills of other fish. It establishes 'cleaning stations', which it advertises with a special swimming 'dance'.

Two of the most attractive and common wrasses in the marine park are the moon wrasse (*Thalassoma lunare*) and the green moon wrasse (*Thalassoma lutescens*), which have a beautiful combination of green, blue, purple and yellow markings. Other common wrasses include the redspot wrasse (*Stethojulis bandanensis*), the nebulous wrasse (*Halichoeres nebulosus*), the clubnosed wrasse (*Gomphosus varius*) which has a very elongated snout, the slingjaw wrasse (*Epibulus insidiator*) which can rapidly shoot the jaws forward to capture prey, the coral pigfish (*Bodianus axillaris*) with its distinctive black spots, the yellowtail wrasse (*Anampses meleagrides*), the tripletail maori wrasse (*Cheilinus trilobatus*) and two larger species, the thick-lipped wrasse (*Hemigymnus melapterus*) and the hump-headed wrasse (*Coris aygula*).

## Parrotfish

Parrotfish (Scaridae) are closely related to wrasses. The distinctive fused teeth enable parrotfish to scrape algae from coral and rock, or eat coral polyps. If you listen carefully when a school is close by, you can hear the crunching and scraping sounds as they feed. You can often see fresh white marks on the reef where parrotfish have been grazing.

*Steephead parrotfish (*Scarus microhinos*). Photo - Bill Brogan*

The large quantities of coral and rock consumed with the algae or polyps are ground up by teeth in the throat, and are excreted as fine sediment. Large clouds of sediment are frequently seen as parrotfish swim by. At night, many parrotfish secrete a mucus 'sleeping bag' that envelops them, and protects them from predators by masking their scent.

Parrotfish are often brightly coloured, particularly in blue, green and turquoise shades, such as the male bridled parrotfish (*Scarus frenatus*). The male and female usually have different colour patterns. The species most easily recognised at Ningaloo Marine Park are the blue-barred parrotfish (*Scarus ghobban*), Schlegl's parrotfish (*Scarus schlegeli*), the surf parrotfish (*Scarus rivulatus*) and the green-finned parrotfish (*Scarus sordidus*).

## Surgeonfish

Surgeonfish (Acanthuridae) are often seen swimming with parrotfish. They have earned their common name from the sharp, scalpel-like horizontal spine or spines on the base of the tail. These spines can be used in defence to slash other fish. A most attractive surgeonfish is the sailfin tang (*Zebrasoma veliferum*), which can erect its huge dorsal and anal fins like a sail. Other common species are the ring-tailed surgeonfish (*Acanthurus grammoptilus*), the convict surgeonfish (*Acanthurus triostegus*), the stripe-faced unicornfish (*Naso lituratus*) and the humphead unicornfish (*Naso tuberosus*).

## Eels

Moray eels (Muraenidae), such as the giant moray (*Gymnothorax javanicus*) and yellow-edged moray (*Gymnothorax flavomarginatus*), live in crevices in the reef. Occasionally eels can be seen swimming freely, particularly the pale freckled moray (*Siderea thrysoidea*). Although they appear to be friendly and curious, resist the temptation to feed them, as even the small individuals have very sharp teeth.

## Catfish

Eel-tailed catfish (Plotosidae) are regularly seen under ledges, both inside and outside the lagoon. They have eight sensory 'whiskers' around the mouth and a long eel-shaped body. The sailfin catfish (*Paraplotosus* sp.) is velvety black with a tall, narrow dorsal fin and is usually solitary. Juvenile striped catfish (*Plotosus lineatus*), however, congregate in large, tightly-packed balls which move as one. Avoid handling these fish. Three sharp spines on their dorsal and pectoral fins are venomous and can cause extreme pain.

## Goatfish

The goatfish (Mullidae) also have sensory whiskers. A pair of whiskers under the chin is used to detect food in the sediment. Common species are the gold-saddled goatfish (*Parupeneus cyclostomus*), the swarthy-headed goatfish (*Parupeneus barberinoides*), the blackspot goatfish (*Parupeneus signatus*) and the Indian goatfish (*Parupeneus indicus*).

## Scorpionfish

Scorpionfish (Scorpaenidae) are found at all depths, but are not regularly seen as they are masters of disguise. All have venomous spines, the most infamous being the estuarine stonefish (*Synanceja horrida*), which has the most venomous dorsal spines of the whole family. Most spectacular in appearance are the lionfish and firefish, such as the red firefish (*Pterois volitans*), which can often be seen pointing its dorsal spines in your direction!

## Rabbitfish

The rabbitfish family (Siganidae) also have venomous spines, and its members are sometimes sarcastically known as 'happy moments', due to the pain they can inflict if inadvertently handled. Underwater, however, they are attractive fish. Those commonly seen include the doublebar spinefoot (*Siganus doliatus*), the golden-lined spinefoot (*Siganus lineatus*), the threespot spinefoot (*Siganus trispilos*) and the black spinefoot (*Siganus fuscescens*).

## Boxfish and pufferfish

In evolutionary terms, boxfish (Ostraciidae) and pufferfish (Tetraodontidae), despite their curious rounded appearance, are among the most advanced families of fish. Boxfish have a rigid outer bony case and small fins, and give the impression of a wind-up toy when they swim. The species likely to be seen are the yellow boxfish (*Ostracion cubicus*) and the spotted boxfish (*Ostracion meleagris*).

Pufferfish have smooth skin containing small embedded spines. They can inflate their bodies by swallowing water, which is thought to deter predators. The fish are highly toxic to eat, but in Japan are considered to be a delicacy and are prepared by special chefs. The stars and stripes toadfish (*Arothron hispidus*) and the narrow-lined toadfish (*Arothron manillensis*) are regularly seen on dives.

Above: *Spotted moray* (Gymnothorax eurostus).
Below: *Ragged-finned firefish* (Pterois antennata). *Photos - Ann Storrie*

*The potato cod (*Epinephelus takula*) is completely protected in Western Australian waters and may not be taken. Photo - Paul Jelley*

# Large coral reef fish

## Rockcods and gropers

Gropers or rockcods are plentiful in the deeper waters. The well known large potato cod (*Epinephelus tukula*) is often curious and will remain close to, or even follow divers. Other members of this family commonly seen are the coral cod (*Cephalopholis miniata*), the black-tipped rockcod (*Epinephelus fasciatus*), the frostback cod (*Epinephelus bilobatus*) and Rankin's rockcod (*Epinephelus multinotatus*). If you are extremely fortunate you will come across the giant in this family, the Queensland groper (*Epinephelus lanceolatus*), which can grow up to three metres long (making it one of the largest bony fish). Although it is a dull, greyish to greenish-brown, it is inspiring to observe a gentle fish with such an immense body mass. Queensland gropers can occasionally be seen inside the reef in the deeper regions.

## Snappers, sweetlips and emperors

Many of the snappers, sweetlips and emperors are found in the lagoon, but occur in larger numbers in deeper waters. The snappers or seaperches (Lutjanidae) are nocturnal predators which feed on fish, crustaceans and molluscs. Most common are the five-lined seaperch (*Lutjanus quinquelineatus*), the blue-striped seaperch (*Lutjanus kasmira*), the black-spot seaperch (*Lutjanus fulviflamma*), the bigeye seaperch (*Lutjanus lutjanus*) and occasionally the attractive juvenile of the chinaman fish (*Symphorus nematophorus*) and, in deeper waters, the red emperor (*Lutjanus sebae*).

*Sweetlip emperor* (Lethrinus miniatus). *Photo - Peter Morrison*

The sweetlips (Haemulidae) have distinct colour patterns, often very different from the juveniles, such as the many-spotted sweetlips (*Plectorhinchus chaetodontoides*), gold-spotted sweetlips (*Plectorhinchus flavomaculatus*), ribbon sweetlips (*Plectorhinchus polytaenia*) and painted sweetlips (*Diagramma pictum*). In the latter, the adult is a plain silvery grey, and only the juvenile could be described as painted! Sweetlips look similar to seaperches, but have extremely thick lips. They are nocturnal and feed on small bottom-dwelling invertebrates.

Emperors (Lethrinidae) are closely related to sweetlips and seaperches, but generally have a more pointed snout and only moderately thick lips. Many are seen around the glass-bottomed boat in Coral Bay, where they are regularly fed. These are the north-west snapper or spangled emperor (*Lethrinus nebulosus*) and the sweetlip emperor (*Lethrinus miniatus*). The yellow-tailed emperor (*Lethrinus atkinsoni*) is also common on the reef.

## Trevallies

Large trevallies are often curious and will circle a diver, either in deep water or shallow parts of the lagoon. The gold-spotted trevally (*Carangoides fulvoguttatus*), bigeye trevally (*Caranx sexfasciatus*) and golden trevally (*Gnathodon speciosus*) are commonly seen. Juveniles of the latter species are bright yellow with vertical black stripes and often attend large fish such as whale sharks, gropers and manta rays.

## Trumpetfish and batfish

Curiously shaped species sometimes catch your eye. What appears to be a long stick floating by is either a trumpetfish (Aulostomidae) or a flutemouth (Fistulariidae). These fish are extremely elongated with a long, tube-like snout. They stealthily creep up on smaller fish and invertebrates and rapidly suck them into their mouths when they get close enough. The trumpetfish (*Aulostomus chinensis*) has both a bright yellow and a brown colour form. The smooth flutemouth (*Fistularia commersinii*) is more slender than the trumpetfish, with a long thin tail filament, and is a greenish-brown colour.

Occasionally you get the feeling of being observed from above. When you look up you may see a school of large fish shaped like dinner plates, known as batfish (Ephippidae). Most commonly seen are the curious, round-faced batfish (*Platax teira*).

## Sharks and rays

Larger sharks and rays are regularly seen outside the reef in deeper water. These include the grey reef shark (*Carcharhinus amblyrhynchos*), tawny nurse shark (*Nebrius ferrugineus*) and white-tipped reef shark (*Triaenodon obesus*). Fortunately, these large sharks are usually more frightened of you than you are of them and it is a rare privilege to get a good view of one before it swims off into the blue. Many visitors to the Ningaloo Marine Park are delighted to see the majestic manta ray (*Manta birostris*). These large rays are usually on the outside of the reef and are relatively common in these waters. They are harmless filter feeders and graceful swimmers. You can often see suckerfish or remoras attached to manta rays, sharks and other large fish. The suckerfish have a large sucking disc on top of the head with which they can attach themselves to larger fish. These 'hitchhikers' benefit from feeding on scraps of food dropped by the host, or feed on skin parasites.

Above: *The yellow colour form of the painted flutemouth* (Aulostomus chinensis). *Photo - Sue Morrison*
Below: *Manta rays* (Manta birostris) *are harmless filter feeders. Photo - Simon Jones*

Large sharks are rarely seen inside the reef, but younger individuals are sometimes present. More frequent are the bottom-dwelling wobbegongs that rest under ledges during the day, and rays such as the blue-spotted fantail stingray (*Taeniura lymma*) which often hides in the sand with just its eyes exposed.

# Whale sharks

Ningaloo Reef has become famous all over the world for its population of whale sharks. Each year, these sharks migrate inshore to the Ningaloo Reef shallows, which allows people the privilege of a close look at these magnificent fish. The whale shark (*Rhincodon typus*), in the Family Rhincodontidae, is the largest fish (a true shark, not a whale) in the ocean and the largest cold-blooded animal in the world. The biggest specimen ever measured was 12.18 metres long, weighed 11 tonnes and had a mouth 1.36 metres wide! Despite their huge body mass, whale sharks are harmless filter-feeders.

## Appearance

These beautiful animals have a distinctive checkerboard pattern of white spots and stripes, with a dark bluish-grey background on the upper surface. The undersurface tends to be pale, without markings. Small fish, such as remoras, pilot fish and juvenile golden trevallies are frequently seen in attendance, swimming very close to the body surface, or even inside the mouth of the whale sharks.

The head of the whale shark is different from other sharks, being very broad and square in shape. The wide mouth is positioned at the front of the head. Sensory cells in

*Tawny nurse shark* (Nebrius ferrugineus). *Photo - Vivien Matson-Larkin*

*Snorkellers can usually keep up when the whale sharks are swimming slowly. Photo - Ann Storrie*

the nasal grooves above the mouth can detect food in the water. The eyes are very small and situated behind the angle of the jaw. The spiracle (vestigial gill slit) is the round hole just behind the eye. There are five large gill slits on each side close to the pectoral fins. Along each side of the body are three prominent ridges. The lateral line (sensory groove which can detect vibrations) runs along the sides of the body below the second ridge.

## Distribution

Whale sharks are found throughout the world's tropical and warm temperate seas and a small number (approximately 200 to 400 individuals) are seen off Ningaloo between March and early June every year. Their appearance is possibly linked with the annual coral spawning and with the spawning of many other invertebrates in this region. This provides a rich planktonic 'soup' for whale sharks to feed on, as well as numerous other small marine animals, such as small fish and squid, which are attracted to feed on the spawn. It is not known where the Ningaloo whale sharks spend the rest of the year. It could be that they move just offshore to deeper waters below the level of the continental shelf, or that they migrate for greater distances around the oceans. Tagging programs have been implemented recently, which should provide information on their migration patterns in the near future.

## Feeding

Whale sharks have very large gill slits which are adapted for filtering: they contain a spongy tissue formed from modified denticles. The sharks filter planktonic and nektonic (active) organisms including crustaceans (krill, copepods, crab larvae), squid, jellyfish and small fish. They can filter feed either actively or passively. In passive feeding, the whale shark swims with the mouth open in a normal gape. When actively feeding, the mouth is widely distended and the shark searches out concentrations of plankton to swim through, sometimes moving the head from side to side. Whale sharks can also suck food-rich water through the mouth; they can occasionally be seen doing this at the surface in a vertical position. Active feeding enables sharks to capture the faster-moving prey, but it filters smaller volumes of water when doing this and therefore less of the small plankton is filtered. A combination of active and passive feeding methods therefore allow whale sharks to capture all sizes of planktonic and nektonic prey. Despite being filter feeders, whale sharks still possess teeth. Adult whale sharks have more than 3000 small teeth, between 1.5 and 4.5 millimetres long, arranged in about 300 rows. These are thought to prevent larger food items slipping out of the mouth.

## Reproduction

Since a female whale shark was harpooned off eastern Taiwan in July 1995 with 300 almost full-term embryos in her uterus, it is now known that whale sharks give birth to live young. The smallest free-swimming whale sharks found have been 40 to 50 centimetres long, but very few of these have been seen. Individuals of 3.5 metres or more are found throughout the world, in a band extending about 30° on either side of

*Juvenile golden trevallies and remoras (sucker fish) often accompany whale sharks. Photo - Sue Morrison*

*The mysterious whale shark* (Rhincodon typus). *Photo - Sue Morrison*

the Equator. Scientists are uncertain when the onset of sexual maturity occurs, but the only sexually mature male observed at Ningaloo was an estimated nine metres long. These sharks are extremely difficult to age, but it has been suggested that they become sexually mature at around 30 years and have a possible life span of 100 years.

## Protection

The long time taken to reach maturity, and therefore for reproduction to occur, indicates how vulnerable these massive fish are. Even a small decline in their numbers could dramatically affect their reproductive potential. Another problem is that so little is known about their biology and population numbers that we do not know if whale shark numbers are in decline or not. We must make every effort to protect and study whale sharks so as to preserve them for the future, for all to enjoy.

## Observing whale sharks

Regulations about how to approach and behave around whale sharks have been set out by the Department of Conservation and Land Management (CALM). Charter boat operators will inform you about what you can and can't do when observing whale sharks. Those fortunate enough to meet a whale shark in the water will have the experience of a lifetime!

Many more species of fish occur in the Ningaloo Marine Park, but cannot all be covered here. See the field guides listed in the bibliography for more information.

# Cold blooded!

*The ocean seems no place for cold blooded animals that breathe air. But two types of reptiles – turtles and sea snakes – boast some remarkable adaptations that enable them to thrive in the water.*

## Turning turtle

Amazingly, marine turtles have survived for around 150 million years, and have changed little from that time to today. It is ironic that all seven species of turtles that inhabit our oceans are now considered to be threatened or seriously endangered. Many countries have passed laws to protect turtles and ban the import and export of their products.

The green turtle (*Chelonia mydas*) is the most common species of turtle and can be seen anywhere within the Ningaloo Marine Park. If you are lucky, you may see several during one dive on the outer reef. Despite its name, the green turtle is actually a greyish-brown to black colour. The green actually refers to the colour of its fat, which was evident when the animal was boiled to make soup. Although green turtle hatchlings are carnivorous, the adults shift to a vegetarian diet. They prefer to graze on seagrass beds and algae.

The loggerhead turtle (*Caretta caretta*) is one of the most endangered species that nests in Australia. This animal grows to around one metre long, and its head is large in comparison to its body. Its diet is mostly shellfish, crustaceans and jellyfish. Unfortunately, turtles can mistake plastic bags for jellyfish. If a bag is eaten, it can block the respiratory or digestive tracts of the turtles and they can either suffocate or starve to death. It is estimated that between 300 and 500 female loggerheads nest in Western Australia each year, predominantly in the Muiron Islands, north of the Ningaloo Marine Park.

The hawksbill turtle (*Eretmochelys imbricata*) may also be seen in Ningaloo Marine Park, especially at Coral Bay. It has a sharp-beaked head and is dark coloured on both body surfaces.

## Nesting

Green turtles are particularly active in this area during the nesting season between October and February. During this time, the females lumber onto the beach to deposit up to 150 eggs. The eggs

Left: *Adult green turtle.*
*Photo - Bill Brogan*
Right: *Green turtle hatchling.*
*Photo - Ann Storrie*

are laid in a hole excavated by the female with her flippers. It is a laborious task that sometimes takes several hours, or even a few nights if the female changes her mind about the site she has chosen. She may also be disturbed by enthusiastic people watching her progress. If you do turtle watch, do not disturb the female until she has begun laying her eggs. She can then be approached and photographed quietly.

The young hatch after about two months of incubation. They usually leave their sandy nests at night to avoid numerous predators such as birds, lizards, crabs and foxes. When the baby turtles reach the water, they then have to contend with sharks, large fish and birds that hunt at the surface. It is estimated that, even under natural conditions, only five per cent of hatchlings from a single clutch will reach the open ocean. Even then, the chances of survival are so small that probably no more than one female from each clutch will survive to sexual maturity.

If you find a turtle, please give it the respect it deserves. Don't ride it or disturb it as it searches for a nesting place. If it has a tag, note the number and contact the Department of Conservation and Land Management, which is conducting a turtle tagging and research program. Your find may add to our knowledge of these creatures, as one newly-born loggerhead turtle did recently in the Sargasso Sea. The seagrass grazing grounds of the Sargasso Sea lie at least 1000 kilometres from the nearest islands on which the turtle could have nested!

## Snaking through the water

The seas of Australia support about 32 of the world's 55 known species of sea snakes. Being cold blooded animals, most sea snakes are confined to tropical and sub-tropical waters. Individuals occasionally stray into the temperate zones, where they eventually

*Green turtles mating. Photo - Paul Jelley*

*Sea snakes, such as this olive sea snake, are occasionally seen on the outer reef. They are usually very docile but can be quite inquisitive of divers. Photo - Ann Storrie*

perish in the cooler waters. Sea snakes are occasionally seen on the outer reef of the Ningaloo Marine Park and in Exmouth Gulf, but are rarely found inside the reef.

Sea snakes are closely related to terrestrial snakes, but are easily distinguished by their paddle-shaped tails and valves in their nostrils. Like turtles, they must surface at regular intervals to breathe air. The average submerged time is about 30 minutes, however, some have survived for up to five hours without breathing. This may be partly due to their ability to absorb small amounts of oxygen through their skin. Sea snakes give birth to live young in the sea.

Most sea snakes feed on small fish and eels. Some, however, are quite specialised and have adapted to a diet of fish eggs, while others feed mainly on prawns. The potency of sea snake venom facilitates the quick death of prey, which is necessary if the snake is to find its victim again in the underwater environment. It is unlikely that the venom was ever meant primarily for defence. In fact, some statistics indicate that if a sea snake does bite to defend itself, it only injects venom about 30 per cent of the time.

Sea snakes are usually quite docile towards people, unless disturbed during the mating season. If a sea snake approaches you, don't panic. Stay still and allow the snake to move past you, which is exactly what most will do. Occasionally, a snake may be inquisitive, especially if it is an olive sea snake (*Aipysurus laevis*). These large snakes can attain a length of two metres. They are common in Australian waters and a subspecies lives as far south as Shark Bay. These snakes are usually very tolerant of divers. They may even approach to 'taste' the diver's wetsuit with their forked tongue. This is the sea snakes' most efficient way of examining other creatures underwater, because, despite many of their fantastic adaptations to the marine environment, they were given terrestrial eyes. They see as we would underwater without a mask!

# Having a whale of a time

*Like their terrestrial relatives, all marine mammals are warm-blooded, have lungs with which to breathe air and give birth to live young that are suckled with milk secreted by mammary glands.*

There are 76 species of whales and dolphins in the world's oceans. They belong to the Order Cetacea. Whales and dolphins are divided into baleen whales and toothed whales. Baleen whales have horny plates called baleen instead of teeth. Their food, which consists of plankton, small invertebrates and very small fish, is strained through these plates. The toothed whales include dolphins and porpoises, which actively hunt for fish, squid and other animals.

## Whales

There are 33 species of whales in our oceans, and several of these migrate along the Western Australian coast. The blue whale, the largest animal that has ever lived on Earth, travels through deep waters well offshore. Others, such as the humpback whale, are more coastal in their habits and are frequently seen close to the outer reef at Ningaloo.

Humpbacks are baleen whales with knobby heads, very long flippers and a humped back with a small dorsal fin. Each autumn, humpback whales leave their feeding grounds in Antarctica to migrate along Australia's eastern and western coasts to calve in northern waters. They return in spring. It is estimated that up to 4000 individuals migrate along the western coast each year. During the northward journey, the whales are intent on their route, rarely deviating, and staying well out to sea. On their return, however, they take their time, stopping in various bays along the coast, where they put on spectacular displays of breaching, rolling, slapping and generally having a 'whale' of a time. Their procrastination during the return journey is probably to enable the newly-born calves time to grow and develop a thicker layer of blubber for protection in the cold feeding waters surrounding Antarctica.

Left: *A humpback whale.*
Right: *Humpback whale tail.*
*Photos - Doug Coughran*

Humpback whales are noted for their vocalisations. Males may sing for up to half an hour at a time during the breeding season. The gestation period is about 12 months and the calves weigh up to two tonnes when born. The calf may consume 600 litres of milk per day. By the age of 11 months, when the calves are weaned, they may be up to nine metres long. Like many whales, the females are larger than the males. The females' average length is around 15 metres, whereas the males are about 14 metres.

The best months of the year to see humpbacks in the Ningaloo Marine Park are from August to October. Whale watching tours are organised from Coral Bay and Exmouth and are conducted according to a code of ethics. Vessels should not approach any closer than 100 metres to a whale. If an animal approaches a vessel, the engine should be put into neutral until the animal has passed. Swimming with whales is not permitted and it is an offence to harass whales.

One of the more unusual sights that can be seen on a whale watching trip is a humpback whale standing on its head, with its tail sticking three to four metres into the air. The female whale may stay in this position for up to two hours. It is thought to be a way of discouraging male suitors!

# Dolphins

The most common dolphin found in the Ningaloo Marine Park is the bottlenose dolphin (*Tursiops truncatus*) and it is also the species most inclined to interact with people. The famous Monkey Mia dolphins of Shark Bay are bottlenose dolphins. One of the most distinctive features of the bottlenose dolphin is its clearly defined, relatively short, thick beak. It has a grey back, with a paler flank and belly. Its dorsal fin is prominent, with a slight hook, and is set mid-way along the body. Bottlenose dolphins vary considerably in size. The animals at Shark Bay and Ningaloo average about three metres in length, but those in Perth waters can be around four metres. The species lives for 25 to 30 years and calves every two to three years.

The bottlenose dolphin is found throughout the world, except in the coldest waters, and there appear to be distinct inshore and offshore groups. Those that live near the coast usually form groups of between 10 and 50 animals, whereas those living offshore have up to several hundred in a pod.

Bottlenose dolphins are very active. They will ride the bow waves of ships, surf ocean waves and coastal breakers, and are capable of leaping up to six metres out of the water. They can dive several hundred metres in search of food, which usually consists of squid, fish and octopuses. Unfortunately, they sometimes strand on beaches, either individually or in small groups. If you find a stranded dolphin, contact the Department of Conservation and Land Management immediately and, if possible, keep the animal wet and shaded, as sunburn is often the major cause of scarring and death.

Another species frequently seen at Coral Bay and within the Ningaloo Reef is the Indo-Pacific humpbacked dolphin (*Sousa chinensis*). This small dolphin, often less than three metres long, has, as its name suggests, a humped back. It often forms small groups or may even be seen alone or in pairs swimming with bottlenose dolphins. The humpbacked dolphin, however, prefers shallow waters within the reef and is less active, rarely riding bow waves of boats.

The best place to view bottlenose and humpbacked dolphins is in the sandy area between the shore and the reef between Coral Bay and South Passage. Common

Above: *Indo-Pacific hump-backed dolphins in the shallows of Ningaloo Marine Park.*
*Photo - Doug Coughran*
Below: *Bottlenose dolphins. Photo - Ann Storrie*

dolphins, which have a characteristic hourglass pattern of light grey and tan or yellow on their sides, and a dark stripe from flipper to lower jaw, may also be seen in this area. Several other species, such as Risso's dolphins, spotted dolphins and common dolphins may be seen well offshore.

# Dugongs

An encounter with a dugong is an unforgettable experience. Unfortunately, few people have had the pleasure of seeing these shy, gentle marine herbivores. They belong to the Order Sirenia, which also includes three species of manatee. They look a little like a rotund dolphin, yet they are more closely related to elephants. One theory suggests that a sea cow, which descended from an ancestor shared by elephants, fed on seagrass meadows in the Eocene period (54 to 38 million years ago). This was the ancestor of modern manatees and dugongs.

Despite mythical legends relating dugongs to mermaids, the dugong has not had a happy relationship with people. It has been hunted for thousands of years for its meat, oil and tusks, and more recently it has been a victim of fishing nets. This, coupled with depletion of seagrass meadows and an extremely low reproductive rate, has led to the world-wide decline of the species. Dugongs are not rare in northern Australia, but they are given special protection under WA's Wildlife Conservation Act. A large population of around 10,000 is estimated to live in Shark Bay and about 2000 inhabit Exmouth Gulf and the Ningaloo Reef area.

Dugongs may be found alone, as cow-calf pairs, or in herds of up to several hundred. They can live for up to 75 years. Females give birth to a single calf only every three to

*There are about 2000 dugongs in the Ningaloo Marine Park. Photo - Vivien Matson-Larkin*

*A dugong sanctuary has been proclaimed at Bruboodjoo Point. Photo - Vivien Matson-Larkin*

seven years, and it takes 10 years for the young to reach maturity. When fully grown, the dugong measures two to three metres in length and can weigh up to 400 kilograms.

The best place to see dugongs in the Ningaloo Marine Park is in the shallow waters just west of Point Maud and further north off Bruboodjoo Point, which is a dugong sanctuary.

# References and recommended reading

Abbott, R T & Dance, S P. 1982. *Compendium of Seashells*. E.P. Dutton, Inc. New York.

Allen, G R. 1997. *Marine Fishes of Northern Australia; A Field Guide for Anglers and Divers*. Western Australian Museum, Perth.

Allen, G R & Swainston, R. 1988. *The Marine Fishes of North-Western Australia*. Western Australian Museum, Perth.

Allen, G R & Steene, R. 1994. *Indo-Pacific Coral Reef Field Guide*. Tropical Reef Research, Singapore.

Colman, J. 1998. *Whale Shark Interaction Management with particular reference to Ningaloo Marine Park*, CALM, Perth.

Cresswell, G R. 1991. *The Leeuwin Current - observations and recent models*. Journal of the Royal Society of Western Australia. Volume 74.

Dakin, W J & Bennett, I. 1987. *Australian Seashores*. Angus & Robertson Publishers, New South Wales.

Department of Minerals and Energy. 1997. *Geology of the North-West Cape*. Fact Sheet 23. Department of Minerals and Energy, Western Australia.

Fautin, D G & Allen, G R. 1992. *Field Guide to Anemonefishes and Their Host Sea Anemones*. Western Australian Museum, Perth.

Gosliner, T M, Behrens, D W & Williams, G E. 1996. *Coral Reef Animals of the Indo-Pacific*. Sea Challengers. Monterey, California.

Hutchins, J B. 1994. *A Survey of the Nearshore Reef Fish Fauna of Western Austalia's West and South Coasts – The Leeuwin Province*. Records of the Western Australian Museum, Supplement No: 46.

Hutchins, J B & Swainston, R. 1986. *Sea Fishes of Southern Australia. Complete field guide for anglers and divers*. Swainston Publishing, Perth.

Jones, D & Morgan, G. 1994. *A Field Guide to Crustaceans of Australian Waters*. Reed, Chatswood, New South Wales.

*The Ningaloo Marine Park offers superb diving. Photo - Ann Storrie*

Karniewicz, R. 1994. *The Whale Sharks of Ningaloo Reef: A booklet of interpretive materials for guides and tour operators in the whale shark interaction industry.* In National Ecotourism Strategy, Commonwealth Department of Tourism. Australian Government Publishing Service.

Marsh, L M. *Report on selected marine invertebrate fauna of Ningaloo Reef,* compiled for CALM, unpublished.

Marsh, L & Slack-Smith, S. 1986. *Sea Stingers - and other venomous and poisonous marine invertebrates of Western Australia.* Western Australian Museum, Perth.

Pearce, A & Cresswell, G. 1985. *Ocean Circulation off Western Australia and the Leeuwin Current.* CSIRO Division of Oceanography. Perth, Western Australia.

Prince, R I T. 1996. *Western Australian Marine Turtle Project.* Department of Conservation and Land Management, Western Australia.

Sheppard, C & Wells, S M. 1988. *Coral Reefs of the World.* Volume 2: Indian Ocean, Red Sea and Gulf. United Nations Environment Programme. International Union for Conservation of Nature and Natural Resources.

Simpson, C J, Cary, J L & Masini, R J. *Destruction of Coral and Other Reef Animals by Coral Spawn Slicks on Ningaloo Reef WA.* Coral Reefs 12: 185-191.

Simpson, C J & Masini, R J. *Tide and Seawater Temperature Data from the Ningaloo Reef Tract WA.* EPA Perth WA Bulletin 253.

Swainston Publishing, 1998. Laminated waterproof underwater fish guide for tropical Australia. Two double-sided pages, covering 110 species.

Taylor, G. 1994. *Whale Sharks.* Angus and Robertson Publications. Sydney, Australia.

Thomson, C. 1997. *Discovering Shark Bay Marine Park and Monkey Mia.* Department of Conservation and Land Management. Western Australia.

Veron, J E N. 1986. *Corals of Australia and the Indo-Pacific.* Angus and Robertson Publishers, Sydney, Australia.

Veron, J E N & Marsh, L M. 1998. *Hermatypic corals of Western Australia: records and annotated species list.* Records of the Western Australian Museum, Supplement No. 29.

Wells, F E & Bryce, C W. 1993. *Sea Slugs of Western Australia.* Western Australian Museum, Perth.

Wilson, B. 1988. *Range to Reef.* Department of Conservation and Land Management, Western Australia.

# Index

*A common starfish* (Pentagonaster duebeni).
*Photo - Vivien Matson-Larkin*

*Bicolor blenny. Photo - Ann Storrie*

2003463-1003-5M